From the
BOTTOM
to the
TOP

From the BOTTOM *to the* TOP

CONQUERING OPPOSITION:
NAVIGATING THROUGH ACCELERATION

JERRY K. ADDY

FOREWORD BY BISHOP CALVIN B. LOCKETT

From the Bottom to the Top
Conquering Opposition: Navigating through Acceleration

Copyright © 2019 by Jerry K. Addy

For information contact us at: www.jerryaddyministries.org

DEDICATION

THIS BOOK IS DEDICATED TO MY WONDERFUL wife of over sixteen years, Shanté Addy. She has been and continues to be an incredible source of support and sanity for me as I've experienced God's process of navigating acceleration over the years. She has celebrated my accomplishments publicly and has spoken life to me during my private failures. *From the Bottom to the Top* is a testament of her diligence in praying for me over the course of our marriage and service in ministry. Thank you for all the years of prayer, intercession, and love!

To my children, Nathan, Royalty, and Trinity. I am grateful to God for each of you and extremely proud to be your father! As you engage life, I pray you will continue to grow in wisdom, knowledge, and understanding! I know your best days are ahead of you because the foundation in Christ has been laid. I love each of you dearly!

CONTENTS

FOREWORD

I AM PRIVILEGED AND HONORED TO WRITE THE foreword to this book—not exclusively because of its content but because I saw its pages unfold before my very eyes. The words "From the Bottom to the Top" could easily have been "From the Back to the Front!" Elder Addy joined Christ the Healer Church sixteen years ago as a broken young man who had gone through one of the most difficult times in his life. I often remind him of how he'd sit at the back of the church and listen to the Word in search of a deeper relationship with the Lord Jesus Christ. I've watched his tragedies become triumphs and his setbacks become steppingstones that ordered his steps to the place the Master ordained him to be.

From the Bottom to the Top is not a book that boasts about the successes of Elder Addy. Conversely, it spotlights the pilgrimage of the Biblical patriarch Joseph—one of the Bible's most amazing success journeys. Elder Addy explains how The Lord orchestrated and guided every phase of Joseph's life—from the pit, to Potiphar's house, to prison, to the palace. At the same time, Elder Addy ingeniously connects the life of Joseph with the life of Jesus, the greatest person to ever walk the face of the earth. His comparison and fresh perspective on the life of Joseph will encourage and inspire you to embrace the Christian saying that "there's no secret what God can do . . . what He did for Joseph, He'll do for you!"

In closing, I highly recommend that you *add From the Bottom to the Top* to your library. I encourage you to read it slowly and devotionally. Meditate on its principles. It could very well be one of the best books that you've ever read!

Bishop Calvin B. Lockett
Senior Pastor, Christ the Healer Church in Clarksville, Tennessee
Bishop of Fellowship Relations, Full Gospel Baptist Church
Fellowship International

ACKNOWLEDGMENTS

FIRST AND FOREMOST, GOD HAS REMAINED A constant in all that gave birth to this book. I'm grateful for His consistency, grace, and favor!

I want to give honor to my mother, Georgia Davies, for the years she devoted to my development. I thank God for my late father, Jubson Addy, for without him, I would not be. To my dad, Albert Davies, I am grateful for all the years of conversations filled with wisdom. Words cannot convey how indebted I am to my spiritual mother and mentor, Prophetess Marcia Morrison. She has challenged me and poured into me from the moment we met. I am better as a result of your strength and guidance over the years. Thank you!

I am beyond thankful for Bishop Calvin Lockett, Senior Pastor and Founder of Christ the Healer Church in Clarksville, Tennessee. His unwavering faith and diligence in prayer have been and continue to be instrumental in my life. I am a product of his obedience to God and overwhelmingly proud to call him my pastor! If you know his testimony, then you know him to be a man of great faith and fervently righteous prayer. A special thank you to Pastor Shamond Scales, Senior Pastor of the Zion Church, Jackson, Tennessee, for prophetically sharing God's intent concerning this book during an altar call in 2012.

As far as tributes and acknowledgements, here's to you as well! Yes, that's right! I want to acknowledge your desire to achieve success despite opposition and the trials you've faced in life. Seasons of difficulty are unique because their foundation is to give way to an initial desire to quit. Those seasons beckon us to cease to believe in the potential for breakthrough. The blessing during seasons of adversity is rooted in the process of development we encounter through prayer. Ironically, the opposition we face may trigger a desire to give up, but that opposition is the very thing God uses to guide us toward destiny.

I want to commend your resolve to seek a means of victory as you endure personal battles within acceleration. Every challenging season brings mental fatigue, isolation, and at times, feelings of doubt. The fact that you are reading this book reveals you have not given up on your place of promise. Remain focused on the place of success God designed for you to achieve. No matter the depths of pain you may feel, keep pursuing the top! Most importantly, when you arrive at the top, reach back to help someone that may be where you are currently—simply going through the journey. See you at the top!

INTRODUCTION

FROM THE BOTTOM TO THE TOP WILL ACT AS a blueprint concerning acceleration, navigating opposition, and embracing your life's journey to success. We have all heard the quote, "When life gives you lemons, make lemonade." Although the intent is well meaning, the reality of the process itself still presents a measure of difficulty. To arrive at the satisfaction of ice-cold lemonade, there is the reality (process) of the lemon being cut, then squeezed. In a similar fashion, life presents trials and obstacles as a tool of processing for advancement. It's fair to say that every experience and encounter breeds its share of lessons-learned from dealing with opposition.

Opposition can exist in any area of our lives. It is highly possible to encounter opposition or difficulty in dealing with loved ones, coworkers at all levels, and even those we worship with in ministry. Opposition can present itself through internal insecurities or fears. Often the process to success or your place of promise is difficult and comes with limited instructions on how to navigate the journey effectively. *From the Bottom to the Top* will shift your perspective of the process due to the principles found within each chapter. Continue reading and see for yourself.

Although you may have overcome your past trials, life guarantees you will encounter more obstacles. This book will provide you with new insight(s) to approach overcoming trials and obstacles. Each chapter concludes with a prayer of declaration specific to the issues within each chapter. Several concepts on prayer and intercession will be embedded within each chapter in order to reveal the importance of remaining connected to the Source of your success. Prayer and intercession will prove vital during moments of proving during acceleration. You will also find that simply surviving or overcoming trials is not enough. The underlying theme throughout the pages of this book involves maximizing your trials through intercession. It involves embracing a difficult process in order to achieve a promise. It speaks toward the blessing of momentum in prayer that leads to manifestation.

Maximizing trials may sound self-defeating in context, but I believe you will gain further understanding as you read through each chapter. We will carefully explore how maximizing obstacles can be used to help you achieve success and conquer opposition. Please understand that contrary to popular belief, the term *success* is not limited to financial wealth. It also includes peace, joy, love, happiness, and so on. Biblical success is wholistic. Wholistic biblical success gives life to true contentment and satisfaction. Retaining an open mind and receptive heart toward receiving a new perspective on success will yield fruitfulness.

This is a faith-based book centered on spiritual principles. It also contains practical approaches to handling opposition. My earnest desire is that you will eventually receive tangible results as you pursue the definition of success for your life. For those feeling uneasy about the term *faith-based*, do not be alarmed. Keep reading, and be encouraged and challenged. For those feeling they are at the apex of spirituality as it relates to dealing with obstacles, the chapters will challenge you from a fresh perspective in revelation.

I believe the principles you are about to uncover will usher you into spiritual elevation as well as elevation in the natural. It may sound like a farfetched claim, but I have experienced these principles actively in my walk with God. So much so, the Lord released me to write this book. Some may say, "That was your journey and your situation, so how is it applicable to my life?" The truth of the matter is, you are correct in your statement to a certain extent. However, I believe these same principles can apply to you because God is no respect of person according to Romans 2:11.

The concepts within these pages are directly related to God's Word and His process of accomplishment of His Word. For various reasons I was intentional about leaving out specific names and situations involving personal difficulty. I believe it's not the heart of God to shed light on the shortfalls of others. I believe His intent is to use everything He's given me as a means of comfort and encouragement to those dealing with similar situations but suffering privately.

I've gained firsthand knowledge of these principles throughout my life. Acceleration and extreme measures of progress and opportunity found me throughout various points of my life. While I felt undeserving, it was His plan. As a result, God prompted a dependency upon Him that breathed life to this book. In the US military, God accelerated me through the enlisted ranks within six years. In spite of a 798 point cutoff score for sergeant and staff sergeant, God allowed me to be promoted from E-1 (private) to E-6 (staff sergeant). After seven years of service, it was time to transition from the US military.

In the midst of transition, the favor and grace of acceleration was evident. Within my federal career, during my time as a Department of Army civilian, God allowed me to advance from a GS-3 civilian employee to a chief supervisory analyst (and shortly after, an acting director) in only seven years of civilian service. Currently, I sit in a seat of high-graded advancement and decision-making authority. Lastly, God rapidly progressed me in spiritual growth and title. As I served in ministry, God elevated me from a lay member, to minister-in-training, then minister, and currently to an ordained elder in a matter of five years. Currently, I serve as the Regional Director of Intercessory Prayer for the Central Region within the Full Gospel Baptist Church Fellowship, International.

My boast is not in anything I have done; it rests in Who God is and His Sovereign plan. The Lord has blessed me in numerous ways, and I believe it will be so in your life in spite of any opposing forces. He has favored me in my family, my career, my health, and my finances due to principles found throughout this book and His faithfulness. Make no mistake about it: the previously mentioned areas of blessings came with accelerated progress and prosperity, but they were accompanied by great measures of opposition. This is why I am sure this book will encourage you. I have endured and prayed my way through the difficult and various forces of opposition.

Biblical numerology suggests that at the time of this writing, I was being perfected (the number 7) in my vocation and graced (the number 5) in my ministry calling. The majority of private lessons learned from accelerated success are nestled in each chapter. I encourage you to approach each concept from the understanding that His Word will not return to you void, but it shall accomplish that which He desires (Isaiah 55:11).

Recognize that these biblically based and practical principles apply to your life. He desires the very best for you! As you read through the remaining pages, be encouraged in God's plan for your life, family, and career. You have been destined, designed, and designated by God to go *From the Bottom to the Top!*

Chapter 1
YOUR MOMENT TO ARISE

"Commitment leads to action. Action brings your dream closer."

—*Marcia Wieder*

EVERYONE HAS A UNIQUE SITUATION THAT plagues them. For some it may be financial frustration. For others it may be work-related difficulty. It could be indecisiveness concerning a difficult decision. Regardless of what your bottom looks like now, there is an outcome waiting for you called success! Despite the level of opposition the process to success may bring, it is your time to arise! The issue is not, are you destined to be successful? The question is, are you patient enough to endure the process to obtaining success?

It is evident our desire to reach the top begins with an urge to exceed our current placement in life. Whether you are experiencing a low place, feel you are currently in a good place, or are at your genesis fighting to overcome, there is a pull for more. The pull for more is a call to action on your part. Viewing the lives of some individuals may suggest otherwise, but the previously mentioned point remains an unchanging truth. Everyone is not designed or purposed to become an "overnight success" with a tear-jerking short story to tell. Those instances do occur, but they are the exception and not the norm. However, if you are willing to put forth the effort, over time, you can conquer your bottom and advance toward success with momentum.

Focus in Prayer—See Past the Bottom

It is vital to embrace the reality that everyone's bottom is different. In order to overcome the bottom, you must purpose to respond to the consistent theme of action. Regardless of where we may find ourselves, one of the realities facing us, on the journey to success is the reality of process. The process requires our participation in reaching for destiny. The good news about the bottom is there is nowhere to go from there but up!

The bottom can yield feelings of stagnation, betrayal, lack of resources, internal insecurities, and so on. We must resolve to take our focus off the situation and redirect it toward an outcome that leads to progress. This is how mental momentum is obtained. As I mentioned in the introduction, God desires the very best for you!

> You are called by God to accomplish and be successful!

Connect through Prayer—Fortified by the Source

The Bible states, "Beloved, I pray that you may prosper in all things and be in health, just as your soul prospers" (3 John 1:2). The word *prosper* is *euodoo* in Greek, meaning "to grant a prosperous and expeditious journey." The verse suggests two things we need to pay attention to. First and foremost, it suggests an evident relationship. Relationships cannot be formed where communication is absent. *Beloved* is a term of endearment and reveals a connection. Bishop William H. Murphy, Jr. addresses the necessity of relationship through connecting to God in his book *The Law of Prayer and Intercession*. He states, "Prayer is the pipeline; prayer is the connection that God uses to get that which is in heaven released into the earth realm." (2019, 39).

The evidence of a connection confirms prayer has taken place. On the journey to success, meditation and communion with God will prove vital primarily due to the opposition you are sure to encounter. Prayer will prove to be vital because you will need instructions from the One who holds the blueprint to your life.

Prayer is one of the key actions we must resolve to do while engaging the bottom. Prayer will reveal any internal issues we are facing. It also strengthens us to manage external opposition. Secondly, the scripture shares with us the need to release all limitations. It clearly reveals God's ability to prosper us is unlimited because He wants us to "prosper in all things." It is through prayer that our ability to navigate difficulty is fortified. Through prayer God releases a grace that will prosper us in all things. As the desire to grow in prayer is cultivated, all areas of your life will attract prosperity. As you navigate the process, and its problems, remember to relinquish all limitations.

Alignment in Prayer—Relinquish Limitations

No matter what your bottom says currently, you need to relinquish the limitation. Relinquishing the limitation is another means of acting. Resolve to pray and renounce any negative words spoken about your future or your abilities that do not align with God's Word concerning your life. It does not matter what hindrances you may be facing; the ability to "let go" can launch you into a new perspective on life. Relinquishing limitations is vital to understanding the fact that we are all called to accomplish and achieve success. It is important because it bridges the gap between knowing your abilities and accessing your abilities. A vital step in relinquishing limits is recognizing the anointing God has placed in you. The word *anointing* may seem overwhelming, but it simply suggests the ability to accomplish, meaning God has graced you to achieve.

This fact of knowing your abilities versus actually accessing them is evident all throughout life. Practically speaking, someone may know they can throw a baseball, but their ability to throw a baseball does not confirm they are ready to pitch in the Major Leagues or even at the collegiate level. Pitchers in the Major Leagues prepare by means of rigorous training in order to remove limitations in their ability to throw. Similarly, the call to "prosper in all things" or be successful takes preparation. It involves a process. For most of us, preparation comes in the form of trials and tests. It comes during the bottom or the valley experience. At times, preparation will come and may be rooted in the form of external opposition.

The Plight of Acceleration

The difference between trials and oppositions will become clearer as you continue to read. For now, let's establish trials as moments of testing before or during advancement and opposition as moments of warfare toward progress or elevation. I will periodically reference the lives of Jesus and Joseph throughout this book to bring clarity on dealing with opposition. It will not be an in-depth study, but I intend to highlight their specific approaches to navigating the valley experiences they encountered. When you begin to understand the concept of starting from the bottom and progressing your way to the top, in the midst of opposition coupled with acceleration, both Joseph and Jesus are prime Old Testament and New Testament examples.

Both obtained great positions of influence and authority. They achieved a great deal within a short period of time (acceleration). They were both able to leave a lasting impact and legacy. They were able to accomplish all of that despite their lowly starting points in life. They journeyed from obscurity to notoriety. In other words, they were both able to go "from the bottom to the top" and achieve success in the midst of trials and opposition.

Graced in Prayer—The Ability to Conquer

I firmly believe Jesus and Joseph were able to conquer various forms of opposition through intercession because of God's Sovereign grace and their connection to God. They were graced to conquer opposition through prayer and intercession because of their desire to do His will. They were intentional about acting upon their relationship with Him.

The Bible clearly mentions Jesus "going away" to pray on several occasions. As it relates to Joseph, I believe he possessed a strong prayer life as well. Pharaoh concluded, in Genesis 41: 38, "Can we find anyone else like this man so obviously filled with the spirit of God?" (NLT) Furthermore, the reason for my suspicion is simple: in order for Joseph to receive the foresight he had as a dreamer—to grow in wisdom, accurately interpret the dreams of others, and still show forgiveness to those who betrayed him—he must have been a person of prayer. Obtaining and maintaining our connection to God is critical due to that connection's ability to release us into a place of access.

One of the obvious hindrances to success when the moment to arise occurs is people are often faced with situations where resources seem limited or access seems to be denied. The fact that access is often an issue is a key reality to embrace because everyone's "bottom" is different. The goal is to figure out your placement in the world without succumbing to distractions. We must become intentional in our desire to operate in a posture of focus. In essence, we must form a disregard for anything contrary to the place of promise God spoke.

Meaning, if I am broke, how can I make more money or obtain wealth without my state of lack becoming a hindrance to progress? If I am overweight, how can I get to a place of healthier living or a previous weight goal? If I am single, how do I find contentment during the process of singleness?

Prayer Shifts Circumstances—Purposed Vision

In those situations and many others, we find our current reality does not match our desired destination or vision. Overcoming your present state in pursuit of purpose can be difficult as you carry a God-ordained purpose or vision.

The same held true for Joseph and Jesus. Joseph saw himself in dreams and visions as one of authority. Yet his reality revealed him to be the youngest in the family and one of limited authority. The people of His day attempted to make Jesus a king, but He saw Himself as a servant with a greater purpose. He was destined to be a King that would rule for eternity. The ability to believe in your purpose, and manifest it, while facing dire circumstances is something very few people master. This is why embracing chapter 1's principle is so vital. Resolving in your heart that you are called to success is foundational to obtaining what God has for you.

Arise in Prayer—No Limits in God

No matter how you personally define success, God has the very best planned for you. Embrace the fact that your moment to arise is now. Arise in prayer. Arise in your expectation and faith. Arise from doubt, insecurities, and fear. In the Message Bible's recording of Jeremiah 29:11, God says through the Prophet Jeremiah, "I know what I am doing. I have it all planned out—plans to take care of you, not abandon you, plans to give you the future you hope for."

Meditating and focusing on this fact can transform your life. It can change your perspective as it relates to your abilities. It can empower you to relinquish limitations. The Apostle Paul conveys God's ability to not only exceed our expectations, but also to overcome limitations in Ephesians 3:20. The scripture declares, "Now to Him who is able to do exceedingly abundantly above all that we ask or think, according to the power that works in us . . ." (NKJV).

With that said, don't ever allow others to make you feel guilty for trying to change your current reality. If poverty, a lack of education, or any habitual issue is in your bloodline (or family tree), then be an agent of change by telling the enemy the curse stops here! People who cannot accept your change for the better simply do not understand the purpose God has for you.

Knowing and believing in God's call on your life to arise is a powerful tool in removing and relinquishing limitations. The truth of the matter is there are limitations placed on us by others (limitations that need to be removed and guarded against) and some we place on ourselves (limitations that need to be relinquished). People do not mind if you succeed so long as you are successful within their limitations. Once you attempt to expand past the boundaries they have set for you, prepare for intense opposition. In the midst of opposition, prepare to rely heavily on God. The strength to embrace your moment to arise is released through prayer. The strength you need to conquer opposition is transmitted as you seek the Lord. Psalm 105:4 says, "Seek the Lord and his strength; seek his presence continually" (ESV).

This is exactly what the "Joseph blessing" alludes to when his father pronounced that Joseph's branches would go over the wall [Genesis 49:22] followed by references of attacks by archers [Genesis 49:23]. In all reality, external attacks (a term to classify warfare from opposing forces) should concern us, but self-perceived limitations are the most damaging to our ability to prosper.

Internal limitations are more damaging than external limitations because they directly impact the mind or will. They need to be relinquished through prayer because they are deeply placed in the heart. This is why Proverbs 4:23 cautions us, "Above all else, guard your heart . . ." (NIV). An inability to guard the heart leads to mental fatigue. Mental fatigue exposes our minds to greater levels of mental warfare. It is one thing when others do not believe in you, but it's something else when you do not believe in yourself. A major part of embracing the call to arise consists of working toward relinquishing internal limitations.

The Vitality of Prayer and Intercession—Grasp Purpose

This is why prayer and intercession are so vital. Prayer and intercession change perspective. Prayer and intercession will empower you to see the bottom as a symbol of your beginning and not your final outcome. Prayer and intercession will cause you to realize the bottom is not necessarily a negative place. Through prayer and intercession, your perspective of the valley experience becomes one of processing and not punishment. To fully grasp the desire of God concerning your life and His call to arise out of the valley, there must be a realization of your ability to obtain success.

In simplified terms, you must see yourself worthy of obtaining success. Doing so is an action that brings you closer to your dream. The word *grasp* literally means to "get a hold of mentally." Proverbs 23:7 says, "For as he thinks in his heart, so is he . . ." (NKJV). In other words, whatever you gain a hold of in your internal belief or faith system, you can position yourself to obtain in the natural. Gaining a mental hold of God's desire to make you successful will help you relinquish internal limitations. It will aid you in recognizing and removing external limitations. Although external limitations are not as impactful as internal limitations, they are still problematic to your progress.

The revelation behind removing and relinquishing limitations is very powerful. The absence of limitations in your life unlocks your full potential and releases you to fully receive the plan of God for your life. Confronting limitations through prayer and intercession act as a catalyst. It launches you to a place of greater focus. It's not a place of perfection, but it launches you into a place of unhindered purpose. This principle truth was revealed to Joseph by his father Jacob in Genesis 49:22–26. These verses are commonly referred to as the "Joseph Blessing."

22 Joseph is a fruitful bough, a fruitful bough by a spring; his branches run over the wall. 23 The archers bitterly attacked him, shot at him, and harassed him severely, 24 yet his bow remained unmoved; his arms were made agile by the hands of the Mighty One of Jacob (from there is the Shepherd, the Stone of Israel), 25 by the God of your father who will help you, by the Almighty who will bless you with blessings of heaven above, blessings of the deep that crouches beneath, blessings of the breasts and of the womb. 26 The blessings of your father are mighty beyond the blessings of my parents, up to the bounties of the everlasting hills. May they be on the head of Joseph, and on the brow of him who was set apart from his brothers. (ESV)

Pray Fervently and Cast Your Cares Upon Him—The Blessing is on You

I implore you to receive the "Joseph blessing" as your own. Joseph's life story teaches us many things. One of the most invaluable lessons is that properly managing trials and tests leads to moments of transformation and elevation. As God graces you to arise out of the valley, pray fervently and in faith. Trust the process of cultivation. Regardless of the limitations facing you, recognize they are all subject to God's Sovereignty.

Utilize prayer and intercession to align your priorities with God's priorities. Doing so will cause you to remain fruitful and operate in a posture of humility. Humility is the key to obtaining and maintaining your moment to arise. Humility will foster your ability to thrive. 1 Peter 5:6–7 provides insight to the level of influence living a life of humility carries. The scripture says, "Therefore humble yourselves under the mighty hand of God, that He may exalt you in due time: casting all your care upon Him, for He cares for you" (NKJV).

The call to arise is a clarion call from God to us. It beckons us to a balanced life of humility and productivity. God positioned you to produce in elevation. The call to arise requires we seek God from a posture of submission to receive elevation. The word *exalt* in 1 Peter 5:6 means to elevate literally and figuratively. It suggests a raising to a place of dignity, honor, and prosperity. In essence, God will lift up and exalt you as you submit to Him.

The word *casting* means to throw upon or give up to God. The first mention of "care" in verse 7, in which we are told to cast on God, carries the idea of distractions. It conveys the idea of someone being pulled in different directions. The second mention of "care" in verse 7 reveals God's concern for the matters we face. It literally means "to care about"; if we cast our cares to God through a humble posture of prayer, He not only handles the anxieties we face, but He will exalt us in the midst of difficulty.

Casting all your care on Him through consistency in prayer allows you to remain focused. Dwelling in His presence affirms the capacity to produce and remain in position. Genesis 49:22 says, "Joseph is a fruitful bough, a fruitful bough by a spring . . . ." This alludes to God's intentional placement of Joseph in a location that was not barren, meaning the fact that he was placed by a spring carries significance. It suggests the ability to be fruitful or produce due to being sovereignly placed by God.

Regardless of where you find yourself in life right now, your current situation is designed to refine you as you navigate the journey to success. Remain encouraged in God's placement and pursue His presence. He has empowered you to thrive. God has anointed you for the journey. His will is for you to achieve. That is the essence of the anointing: to accomplish. The bottom simply symbolizes the beginning or infancy stage of a thing. It represents your processing toward purpose. Your moment to arise is about fleeing complacency. Respond to the call through prayer and intercession. God will reveal the bottom is not a negative position, although you may feel uncomfortable or uncertain about your placement. It is the beginning of your next level. It's your time to arise and answer the call!

~*Your Moment to Arise End-of-Chapter Prayer*~

Lord, I thank You for having great intentions toward me. According to Jeremiah 29:11, I set myself in agreement with Your plans to prosper me and not to harm me. I am grateful because You have called me to be fruitful; therefore, I shall be. According to Mark 11:24, I align my desire with Your desire for my life. I receive the grace to arise! I bind, in Jesus's Name, any hindrances and generational curses to the success You have ordained for my life and my family. I loose, decree, and receive Your plan to use me as an agent of prosperity and an agent of change. According to Romans 5:17, I walk in an abundance of grace and righteousness through Jesus Christ. I align my faith with Ezekiel 34:26 and receive the showers of Your blessings upon my life. Lord, I glorify You for all You have graced me to press my way through. I resolve in my mind and my heart to place my hope in You that I may run and not grow weary, walk and not faint according to Isaiah 40:31. I receive the new strength You promised in Your Word. I declare it is my moment to arise. I bind any opposing forces in Jesus's Name and loose the wind of God and its momentum to accomplish Your will. I decree that I shall seek the Lord and His strength according to 1 Chronicles 16:11. I desire to be an agent of spiritual success, financial success, social success, and emotional success. In Jesus's Name, Amen.

Journal the Journey

Chapter 2

OVERCOME AND BE HEALED

_____

"The true leader serves. Serves people. Serves their best interests and in doing so will not always be popular, may not always impress. But because true leaders are motivated by loving concern than a desire for personal glory, they are willing to pay the price."

—*Eugene B. Habecker*

ANYTHING WORTH ACCOMPLISHING REQUIRES sacrifice. The journey to the top is no different. You will be required to sacrifice in numerous ways. The sacrifice of your time, abilities, and resources will be unavoidable. The reality of the journey to the top is that your sacrifice will require service to others. You will be required to serve in uncomfortable environments. The need will arise for you to serve others you do not agree with, on topics you feel strongly about. Take comfort. The aforementioned situations are not meant to discourage you during your journey to the top. They are allowed by God to develop you in the areas of your character and humility.

A true test of character and humility is found in the response of an individual faced with difficulty. Evidence of servant-leadership rests in the ability to remain consistent during trying times. The strength of servant-leadership is nestled in your ability to overcome. The question is, can you encounter opposition that hurts (mentally or emotionally) during service to others yet still trust God for favorable results? Can you serve others when you feel like quitting? Can you perceive that the purpose in the trial is bigger than any discomfort experienced during the trial?

Overcome in Prayer—Cultivate Frequency and Consistency

To align our perception toward overcoming and being healed, we must be willing to embrace the principle of consistency found in 1 Thessalonians 5:17. The scripture admonishes us to "pray without ceasing." "Without ceasing" in the Greek is *adialeiptos*. It means to pray without intermission, incessantly, or uninterruptedly. It is not a matter of time. It's a revelation of frequency and consistency. Praying without ceasing is a matter of continuing without giving way to interruptions or distractions. In other words, praying without ceasing suggests maintaining a level of focus that supersedes any difficult situation.

Consistency in prayer will facilitate the ability to remain. It fosters a strength in servanthood during seasons of strife. Servanthood can yield powerful results in your life, if you are willing to pursue the endurance to overcome through consistent prayer. The pursuit of endurance is provided through your ability to persist in prayer. Consistency in prayer, coupled with opposition or some form of conflict, is a catalyst to reaching destiny. It may sound a little strange, but how you handle conflict ultimately determines the timing of your breakthrough. This is why overcoming the trial and moving forward in healing is so vital.

Opposition is a tool God allows to mature us. It is a catalyst of spiritual growth. Our present obstacles ultimately prepare us. They teach us in the now how to properly handle our place of promise and success. Learning the impactful lessons of now will ensure you are ready for your next! I have experienced this in my walk with God in both my personal and professional life. In other words, it is critical to your success that you learn to leverage difficult moments. It becomes important to learn to pray for your enemies and those that mistreat you no matter their reason. I realize it may be difficult, but doing so is really to your benefit. Jesus alluded to the benefit of overcoming various situations and the results they provide. Read Matthew 5:2–12.

² "Then He opened His mouth and taught them, saying:
³ "Blessed are the poor in spirit, For theirs is the kingdom of heaven. ⁴ Blessed are those who mourn, For they shall be comforted. ⁵ Blessed are the meek, For they shall inherit the earth. ⁶ Blessed are those who hunger and thirst for righteousness, For they shall be filled. ⁷ Blessed are the merciful, For they shall obtain mercy. ⁸ Blessed are the pure in heart, For they shall see God. ⁹ Blessed are the peacemakers, For they shall be called sons of God. ¹⁰ Blessed are those who are persecuted for righteousness' sake, For theirs is the kingdom of heaven. ¹¹ Blessed are you when they revile and persecute you, and say all kinds of evil against you falsely for My sake. ¹² Rejoice and be exceedingly glad, for great is your reward in heaven, for so they persecuted the prophets who were before you."

Some attribute the above passage of scripture, also known as Jesus's sermon on the mount, to a high moral standard of living for a believer. Others suggest it is portraying God's moral perfection in order to reveal the believer's need to depend on God. Without debating biblical theology, I want to draw your attention to the reality of Jesus's words. The sermon consistently speaks of the benefits of overcoming difficulty. It speaks of leveraging difficult moments and calls you blessed as you walk in the grace to do so.

Being able to receive and walk in the ability to overcome past hurt, through prayer, has allowed God to grace me within seasons of acceleration. I believe God will do the same for you! He is not a respect of person, but He does honor biblical principles. The ability to overcome and be healed is a grace God affords us. The Bible says, "For everyone who has been born of God overcomes the world. And this is the victory that has overcome the world—our faith" (1 John 5:4 ESV).

In Jeremiah 30:17, God declares, "I will restore you to health and heal your wounds . . ." (ESV). The grace to overcome and be healed is a promise from God. In order to gain momentum and achieve it, you must be willing to serve consistently during difficulty and embrace the requirement of consistency in prayer.

Momentum in Prayer—Leverage Rejection
Remain Faithful

The momentum is built as you allow God to shift your perspective through prayer. Through the vehicle of prayer and intercession, God will perform triage on you. He will begin to treat your wounds. The grace to overcome and be healed, which you encounter through prayer, will allow you to leverage the rejections of your past. The grace to overcome and be healed that is released to you through prayer will cause you to appreciate your enemies as a means to greater purpose and not a hindrance.

God has blessed me to rapidly excel during my service in the military. He has remained faithful to me through the difficult moments in my federal career by clearing a path of rapid success. His faithfulness was also revealed during my service in His Kingdom. The aforementioned areas were filled with acceleration and prosperity, but they also came with unique measures of opposition. This book is not meant to be a memoir. For that reason, details were intentionally left out.

The point of this written work is not to glorify the difficult or shed light on any individual's (or group's) inability. The point is to reassure you that no matter the depth of the pain from past offenses, you can overcome and be healed by His grace through prayer. Not only will you overcome and be healed as you remain consistent in service and prayer, but God will ensure the breakthrough of abundance will be worth all that you endured.

Clarity was brought to the concept of service during one of several discussions with a close mentor of mine. He explained to me, "Some doors God will open based on your gift, and there are other doors God will open because of your service." Please keep an open mind when it comes to the term *service*. The truth is we all serve in different capacities. We serve in our churches, our families, on our jobs, and even in our social interactions with others. This is embraced by some as the servant-leader model of leadership. Service is not always rewarded with monetary compensation. For example, your service as a parent over the years can yield rewards of your child graduating with honors or simply being a productive member of society. Regardless of the area you "serve" in, one thing for sure is it will be met with opposition and some measure of difficulty.

The most impactful testament you can make during times of opposition is to remain consistent. During the consistency of serving, you will learn who you are and who God is. Learning who you are and who He is will reveal to you a deeper sense of commitment to your assignment and purpose. Your focus will shift from your trial to your testimony.

In other words, there will be less concern as to how difficult things are and more meditation on how great they will be. Bishop Joseph W. Walker III, Presiding Bishop of Full Gospel Baptist Church Fellowship and Pastor of Mt. Zion Baptist Church, wrote a prolific point on opposition in his book *Leadershifts*. He noted the importance of learning from opposition and using it to your advantage. He stated, "Whatever lessons you learn should propel you into your destiny with greater clarity and energy."

> Achieving the promise during seasons of opposition is about learning to guard your faith and your focus.

Guarding your faith and your focus takes place through prayer. Believing that God will fulfill His promises requires faith that is willing to be opposed. Joseph saw his blessing in a dream before it came to be; he held on to the vision in spite of his brothers' attempting to mock and kill him, his father's doubt, and being sold into bondage. Don't allow opposition to cripple your faith. Pursue the grace to overcome through consistency in prayer. It's all part of God's plan and intention to ensure you're spiritually mature enough to handle what He's promised. It's part of His plan to ensure you can handle the fullness of success He has in store.

Persevere in Prayer—Maximize the Opposition

Guarding your faith simply alludes to protecting the ability to persevere and not simply survive. Survival is okay, but it does not help you maximize the opposition. Surviving does not aid you in getting to the top; it simply means you made it through an adverse situation. It does not suggest you came out of the situation in an improved state. God's will for your journey to the top is not survival of opposition; it's perseverance in opposition. Survival denotes achieving averagely or simply maintaining in the same state. In some moments maintaining is all we can do. As I mentioned before, that is okay, and maintaining can be more beneficial than regressing. But as you journey to the top, the pursuit of success requires more than maintaining. This is why we must persist in prayer until perseverance becomes our dwelling place.

A foundational truth to understand about being average is average is not the top. Bishop Joseph Walker III stated in his book *Leadershifts*, "God has not called you to average. Average is being on top of the bottom. He has called you to be on top of the top." If your desire is to go *From the Bottom to the Top,* then you must move past survival into perseverance. View perseverance as the ability to make it through your opposition in an above average state. Perseverance and prayer are the means by which you steadily progress toward purpose. To triage the trials you face, prayer must become a necessity.

Seek God through prayer until you receive treatment for past hurts and offenses. Keep serving others. It is very easy to become bitter when faced with difficult moments in life. The ability to overcome bitterness is found in perseverance. The Bible says it this way: "Therefore, my beloved brothers, be steadfast, immovable, always abounding in the work of the Lord, knowing that in the Lord your labor is not in vain" (1 Corinthians 15:58 ESV). There are moments when God will teach us essential truths concerning our seasons of opposition.

Comprehend in Prayer—Retain Focus and Consistency

Comprehending the purpose behind opposition is important, but it should not be your focus during the season of testing. Retain your focus on Jesus in order to avoid becoming bitter. Learn from the season of testing, but do not dwell on it. Dwelling on it will lead to bitterness. Jesus and Joseph encountered great measures of opposition from various individuals and groups. They encountered opposition from family members, neighbors, religious sects, and political avenues. Yet their responses were to remain consistent in God's assignment.

Joseph's consistent service in the midst of opposition eventually caused him to realize what his brothers meant for evil against him, God meant for good according to Genesis 50:20. Jesus' consistent service in the midst of opposition eventually led Him to a place of further submission—all for the glory of God! Jesus said of Himself in Matthew 20:28 and Mark 10:45 that He ". . . did not come to be served, but to serve . . ." (ESV). Philippians 2:8–9 says,

> [A]nd being found in human form, he humbled himself by becoming obedient to the point of death, even death on a cross. Therefore, God has highly exalted him and bestowed on him the name that is above every name . . .

The previous verses of scripture confirm God's intent to bless the consistency of those that serve. It also validates that remaining consistent in your service is critical to success. Jesus alludes to this in John 12:26 when He states, "If anyone serves Me, let him follow Me; and where I am, there My servant will be also. If anyone serves Me, him My Father will honor" (ESV). The word *honor* in the Greek is *timao,* which means to estimate or fix a value upon. In other words, remaining faithful to God despite difficult times will cause God to place a value upon you that no one can devalue.

God values you regardless of what you are going through. The difference between His value and the value placed on you by others is, the value placed on you by Him will become evident to all. His influence is unmatched by any individual or organization. What God does in your life will be a testament of your maturity and progress. Grow through it! Paul advised his son in the ministry to remain committed and consistent in several areas of life and ministry so that his progress would be evident to all (1 Timothy 4:15). The value God places on us after the test is much greater than the value we receive pre-test. Staying in the mindset of an overcomer is key to your ability to receive the healing you need.

The post-test value speaks to those that tried to discount you. It speaks to those attempting to assassinate your character. When making your way to the top, you must understand it is not on you to help others accept or appreciate your assignment; your job is to guard the assignment. This is why guarding your faith and your focus becomes crucial. The value God places on you will supersede the lies. Instead of contemplating quitting the assignment, rest on the fact that He has qualified you to complete the assignment. Service to God is directly related to your service to others. It's a reflection of your love toward the area or person(s) you serve. Consistency in prayer and intercession cultivates a mindset and will breading momentum. It will establish you and strengthen you to serve during difficulty.

A Love for God in Prayer—No Weight in Intimacy

No matter how difficult the situation, you must resolve in your heart to yield to your love for God. Allow your love for God to speak louder than the desire to give up. Be mindful, God has a way of birthing someone else that is willing to do what we are not. The sovereignty of God oversees the purpose and will of God in the earth. Remember that your life's purpose isn't bound by who supports or believes in you; it is bound by your inability to support or believe in yourself. Overcome the difficult moments by remaining faithful. Build the momentum you need to achieve success by setting aside bitterness and frustration. We will take a closer look at building momentum in chapter 4.

The writer of Hebrews says, "[L]et us lay aside every weight, and the sin which so easily ensnares us, and let us run with endurance the race that is set before us" (Hebrews 12:1). This is more so about effectively running than it is about the race or the fact that you are running. It alludes to making the most of the run by getting rid of unnecessary weight. The same holds true with your journey to the top. You must resolve to get rid of unnecessary weight and distractions.

There were instances in my professional life and walk with God where opposition seemed to come from every angle. Knowing God desired to promote me, I encountered traditional systems that frowned upon the value of education and asking questions. They preferred "yes-men" that operated under a lack of creativity. I was not insubordinate by any means. The issue was my ability to present new concepts caused some to embrace me and others to attempt to hinder me.

The moment you begin to challenge current systems, be ready to encounter opposition. I can recall a time when I decided to further my education in hopes of becoming more marketable for supervisory opportunities. At one point, I was told by a senior leader, "You have the potential, but you are moving too fast," only to never receive a clear understanding of why my youth automatically meant I was not experienced. I obtained the knowledge and attended all the right training(s).

I graduated from various Department of Army schools and attended the Whitman School of Management at Syracuse University for comptroller training. Years later, I was selected for and graduated from the Department of Defense, Defense Civilian Emerging Leader Program (DCELP) cohort 4. I achieved my bachelor of business administration from Austin Peay State University and earned my master's in business administration from Lipscomb University. Not only did I have the training and education, but I had superior performance evaluations as well. This is not mentioned to boast of any of my credentials or accomplishments. Rather, it is meant to highlight although you may meet or exceed the requirements, some systems will attempt to keep you hindered.

Serving in ministry, I encountered hardships from various sources as well. Transparently speaking, the desire to give up crossed my mind on several occasions. I petitioned God to inquire whether my season was up and it was time to transition. I'm sure you can relate. During those moments of weariness, the Holy Spirit would remind me of 2 Timothy 2:12: "[I]f we endure, we will also reign with him" (ESV). The point is you can do all the right things and still encounter opposition.

Tenacity in Prayer—Overcome in Favor

The validity of the previously mentioned point is proven throughout the life of Joseph and Jesus. I'm sure if you evaluate your life, you can attest to the same fact. It is very possible to be God's choice and people deny you access. The most important lesson to be learned: *do not* give up! Overcome and be healed. Do not take past hurts into a promising future. Pray for the strength to keep serving and keep moving according to God's will. The ability to suffer with Him is the qualifier that elevates you to reign with Him.

God is so sovereign in His strategy and plan. At times, He will speak a word of encouragement to you directly. In other moments, a word of encouragement may come through people. To this day, I still have an email Bishop Calvin Lockett (my Pastor of over sixteen years) sent to me during one of the most difficult seasons in my life! It was emailed at 10:38 p.m. on October 2, 2011. Yes, I remember the date and still have the email. That's how rough the season was and how much the email blessed me. It said,

> My dearest son, Minister Jerry Addy, Greetings! I pray that all is well. I wanted to let you know that I love you DEARLY and I'm praying for you. Son, I'm proud of you! But more than that, God is proud of you. Keep doing what you're doing.

Simply put, no matter the opposition, do not give up! The reality of opposition was made clear in Jesus's life from conception. The journey His mother, Mary, and earthly father, Joseph, had to take was a difficult one. When it was time to give birth to the Savior, their attempts to find an available inn were met with rejection. In their time of need, while walking in the plan of God, they were told there was no room for them (Luke 2:6–7 ESV). There are times when people will reject you as you attempt to fulfill God's intended plan for your life. In those moments, choose to stay committed to the promise God has spoken. Do not allow others to distract you by placing their mouths on the process you must endure, especially if they do not have a revelation of your promise.

As you operate in the God-ordained vision for your life, you cannot afford to let rejection become discouragement. When you handle the denial from man the right way, God can force the acceptance. I've experienced this personally and witnessed it in the lives of others. The rejection directed toward you is primarily due to a lack of understanding on their part. Do not take it personal, even if it is personal for them.

When the angel initially appeared to Mary, he confirmed believers can be blessed and highly favored by God and a few verses later be rejected by people. He told Mary in Luke 1:28, "Greetings, O favored one, the Lord is with you" (ESV). By Luke 2:7, she had to lay Jesus in a manger because "there was no place for them in the inn" (ESV). Persecution for righteousness's sake and the rejection you face, occurs based on their lack of insight concerning your future. Overcome persecution through prayer and be healed of every scar.

Persecution for righteousness sake is part of the process of maturity. The biblical concept of being persecuted for righteousness's sake means you are traveling a road less traveled. It comes with fewer friends, less negotiation, and less compromising of the truth. The good news is the same road comes with increased grace to accomplish and achieve. The desire to persevere "in spite of" must become your focus. Perseverance during difficult times will convey your level of loyalty, commitment, and tenacity to God's purpose for your life.

As you journey to the top, God will often remind you that He wired you differently for a reason. Remain loyal as His creation. Conformity may be comfortable and acceptable, but it will damage the God-intent of who you are meant to be in Him. Stay true to God during the trying moments in life by resolving to create praise where there is persecution and creating worship where there is worry.

God will deliver you and honor you just as He did for Jesus, Joseph, and those before you. Hebrews 13:8 declares His consistency. He is the same yesterday, today, and forever. As you remain consistent and choose to guard your faith and your focus despite opposition, God will work on your behalf and take you

From the Bottom to the Top. Keep serving and praying, and you will persevere.

~Overcome and Be Healed End-of-Chapter Prayer~

Lord, I thank you for the grace to serve You. I submit my will for Yours and pray that You would bless the works of my hands in every area of my life. Teach me how to guard my faith and my focus during opposition. I ask that You empower me by Your Spirit to serve those in my family and those I encounter in life. I pray that You would be my Defense and my Refuge during seasons of opposition according to Psalms 59:16. I pray, according to 1 Samuel 12:24, that you would cause me to serve You faithfully and with all my heart no matter the trials I encounter. Thank You for all the great things You have done and shall do! I thank You, Lord. According to Romans 12:11, I will not lack in zeal. I declare I shall keep my spiritual fervor as I serve others and the Kingdom. Lord, I thank you: according to Matthew 23:11, greatness is my portion because I am a servant. I decree that no form of opposition shall derail, distract, or disengage me from the greatness You have promised. I decree and declare healing over my life from every offense. I pray for the grace to walk in humility and gentleness with patience according to Ephesians 4:2–3. I pray that Proverbs 10:12 would be my portion, that I would flee hatred that stirs up strife and dwell in a love that covers all wrongs done against me. I thank You for releasing unto me the anointing to persevere, overcome, and be healed. In Jesus's Name, Amen.

Journal the Journey . . .

_____

_____

_____

_____

_____

_____

_____

_____

_____

_____

_____

_____

_____

_____

_____

_____

_____

_____

_____

_____

Chapter 3

MOTIVE MATTERS: AN ISSUE OF THE HEART

"Motives reveal why we do what we do, which is actually more important to God than what we're doing."

–Joyce Meyer

IN LIFE, IT'S VERY POSSIBLE TO GET CAUGHT UP IN the whirlwind of success. During a ministry conference I attended, I heard a preacher say, "Don't let the platform entice you." In thinking about the statement, I instantly realized the importance of a pure motive. His comment caused me to realize it is possible to pursue greatness only to lose sight of the reason for your diligence. Success can be enticing. Therefore, we must remember that motive matters. God will accomplish great things through your life! He only requires willingness and obedience (Isaiah 1:19).

Contrary to popular belief, the rise to achieving success or any measure of greatness with God requires pure motives. Proverbs 16:2 says, "All the ways of a man are clean in his own sight, but the Lord weighs the motives" (HSCB). It is displeasing to God when He permits elevation or success in the life of a believer, only to witness them lose it due to corrupt behavior or ill motives. It's also displeasing in God's eyes, to give with ill motives. It's as if you haven't given at all.

Evaluate in Prayer—Discern in Accuracy

The Word of God must remain the standard. When it comes to evaluating motives and receiving advice, we cannot solely trust our opinions or the opinions of an individual. The opinions of man

Therefore, it becomes imperative to constantly establish a means of self-evaluation measured by God's word.

are flawed when it comes to spiritual matters. Proverbs 4:23 says, "Above all else, guard your heart, for it determines the course of your life" (NLT). An unguarded heart cannot live a life of pure motives. Neither can an unguarded heart discern if its opinions or the opinions of others are rooted in God. Prayer and meditation on the Word of God are the most effective ways to guard your heart and spiritually discern the motives of others. Jeremiah 17:9 says, "The heart is deceitful above all things, and desperately wicked; Who can know it?"

The Amplified Bible's rendition of Jeremiah 17:9 says, "The heart is deceitful above all things and it is extremely sick; Who can understand it fully and know its secret motives?"

Through prayer and meditation of the Bible, we are able to draw closer to God. God will begin to reveal the hearts, intentions, and motives of others to us by His Spirit. Romans 8:27 says He is "the Father who knows all hearts" (NLT) or "he who searches hearts" (ESV). As a result, God will reveal the motives and intentions of your heart and of others in order to protect His investment in you.

This is why advice and guidance on decisions and opportunities in life should be measured through God's Word. In certain instances, God will send confirmation to you through wise counsel. Their guidance will be centered on His word and not popular opinion. Advice should be welcomed from those that offer wise counsel. The counsel's intent and level of wisdom are revealed through prayer. Pray about the advice, and measure its validity by God's Word. Proverbs 15:22 tells us, "[W]ithout counsel plans fail, but with many advisers they succeed" (ESV).

The Process in Prayer—Patient in Purpose

As you receive counsel during your journey to the top, embrace the reality of the process. It is vital to simultaneously work the waiting process and your faith. Many often struggle with waiting because they neglect the fact that waiting is a critical component to having faith. The scripture declares in Isaiah 40:31, "[T]hey that wait upon the Lord shall renew their strength" (ESV). The reason several individuals are tired and fatigued is because they are trying to self-create the promise that God has spoken.

Some attempt to self-create their "blessing" in faith by justification of their actions, not realizing the wait is a process that involves and testifies of their faith. Do not get me wrong, scripture does inform us faith without works is dead, but there must be balance. Balance occurs when you learn to work what God has instructed, rather than working your own agenda in hopes of helping God do "it" better or faster. I have been there before. There have been moments in my life when I've devised a plan and attempted to place God's seal of approval on it. It happens to the best of us. The resolution comes when you repent in prayer and seek His perfect will.

You are being processed, and God's plan is perfect concerning you. Therefore, learn to trust in Him and His leading above all else. With that said, you must distance yourself from the emotional responses and be willing to ask some difficult questions. There are some things to consider during the process of evaluating motives. For example, have the individuals been properly vetted to offer wisdom to you? Is their motive behind offering advice to you pure?

The length of time you've known them is not a legitimate means of vetting advisors. Truth be told, some people with lastingness in our lives, possess a tainted view when it comes to offering advice. There may be temptation to tell you what you want to hear in fear of possibly losing the relationship. Meaning, in most instances, they will tell you what you want to hear and not what you need to hear. When it comes to your destiny and achieving your purpose, being around for a long time is not a true test of wise counsel. As a result, God's Word should hold precedence as it relates to evaluating motives.

This is relevant to understand because some will work to have their names called, while others work to have their names known. The difference between the two is primarily legacy and a long-term impact. God has called you to be a person of legacy and purpose. The individual who works to only have their name called is often shortsighted. They are not legacy focused. They believe a momentary embrace from someone in authority is most important. They cannot stand to see others receive opportunities of any kind. Guard your heart from becoming like them.

The dilemmas Jesus and Joseph had to navigate were both internal and external. Jesus negotiated His internal battle with God's will in the Garden of Gethsemane and used wisdom to handle external conflict with those who hated Him. Joseph dealt with internal family issues and had to choose to dispel hatred from his heart. He chose not to hold betrayal against those he helped to get out of prison that soon forgot about his kindness toward them.

This is vital to grasp. Accessing and maintaining elevation requires a guarded heart. The heart is a gateway with the ability to direct the course of your life. Proverbs 4:23 affirms the importance of guarding our hearts: "Guard your heart above all else, for it determines the course of your life" (NLT). Solomon Hicks explained in his book *Wise Guys Finish First* that "[g]uarding your heart means keeping some things out, but it also means allowing beneficial things into it." The intensity you use to guard your heart is a foreshadowing of how you will resolve to guard your place of promise.

A guarded heart and a place of focused wisdom is how Joseph could make a statement of forgiveness toward his brothers in Genesis 50:20: "You intended to harm me, but God intended it all for good. He brought me to this position so I could save the lives of many people" (NLT). The same holds true for Jesus: a guarded heart and a place of focused wisdom is how He could forgive those who crucified Him as He declared, "Father, forgive them, for they don't know what they are doing" (Luke 23:34 NLT).

One of the attributes of someone that possesses a guarded heart operating in forgiveness is they carry the mindset of a contender. The lives of Joseph and Jesus directly inform us of this. Their lives reveal accelerated progress and prosperity mandates a willingness to strive during adversity. Meaning, there are seasons where you'll have to contend with Judas. Your rise to the top will require that you eat with him (John 13:27) as a sign of fellowship, embrace a kiss from him on the cheek as a sign of forgiveness, and tell him, "Do what you came to do . . . but do it quickly" (Matthew 26:48–50; Mark 14:44–45). There will also be seasons of transition where you'll be called to part ways. You will be called to carry out the next phase of your assignment, and "Judas" will have to accept his fate. There is no space for betrayal in the next season. Remain vigilant in prayer and carry out the God-assignment on your life.

The God-assignment for your life is preserved and fortified in His covenant nature. Jesus and Joseph encountered opposition during their pursuit of purpose. This informs us that acceleration and favor can breed hatred in the hearts of others. Although we cannot control what others attempt to do to us, we possess total control over our ability to remain focused on completing the journey set before us. Resolving to complete the journey and maintaining the influence God affords us is one of the ways we reveal to God what He says about our destiny matters to us. We convey passion toward the plans He spoke through the prophet Jeremiah (Jeremiah 29:11). It reveals His purpose is essential to us, and we desire to contribute in the manifestation.

Purpose in your heart to become a person of long-term impact. Strive for legacy. Positively impact the lives you come in contact with. Touch their lives that they may touch others. Speak life to others with no hidden agenda. Provide opportunities without a quid pro quo mindset. The arrival to the top is made most impactful when the internal goal and motive is to provide opportunities to those that are currently where you once were. That is the essence of discipleship. True biblical discipleship moves you into servant-leadership in order to empower others.

The importance of the aforementioned evaluation is why the Psalmist petitioned the Lord in Psalms 26:2. He said, "[P]ut me on trial, LORD, and cross-examine me. Test my motives and my heart" (NLT). The truth of the matter is whatever motivates you carries the possibility of being able to define you. That's why your motive must remain pure.

Purity in Prayer—Ascertain Heaven's Agenda

The vehicle of prayer is a means to ensure your motive remains pure. Only the purest of motives stands the test of opposition. Joseph was favored, but don't miss the fact that he kept his heart right and his motive pure. Striving toward both will make the plan of God for your life unstoppable! A pure motive directs your full attention and resources toward progress and not greed. Purity of motive distinguishes between the pursuit of progress and the push for greed.

Evidence of this is found in Matthew 16:20–23. Jesus chose to share a transparent moment with His disciples. He disclosed to them the truth behind His purpose and assignment while on earth. He mentioned the suffering, rejection, and even death He had to endure—all due to His assignment as Redeemer and Savior. After this discourse, Peter (one of His closest disciples) decided to speak against what Jesus told them. Peter said, "Far be it from You, Lord; this shall not happen to You" (Matthew 16:22 NKJV).

Some suggest various reasons behind Peter's denial of Jesus's assignment. Some suggest it was emotional, others purely spiritual, others demonic, and some say all of the above. Regardless the reason, Jesus's response to Peter reveals to us wise counsel is not always found in those closest to us or those that have been around the longest. Jesus replied, "[F]or you are not mindful of the things of God, but the things of men." Jesus concluded and alluded to Peter's motive behind his statement not being in sync with God's plan for His life.

The ability to discern Peter's motive can be accredited to Jesus's consistency in prayer. Prayer allows us to ascertain the pulse of Heaven's agenda. Consistency in prayer has the potency to launch us into a place of knowledge and understanding of spiritual things. As we evaluate our motives and the motives of those around us, we must be careful to do so through prayer. Too often we allow "loyalty" to become a distraction when evaluating motives. The vehicle of prayer and the Word of God must hold precedence in our lives as we navigate discernment of motives and making key decisions.

Prayer is a means of ascension and unlocking access. Bishop William H. Murphy, Jr. reveals the importance of prayer in connection with obtaining the breakthrough in his book *The Law of Prayer and Intercession*. He states,

> Prayer is what locks you into the will of God. What you are looking for and what you need for breakthrough has its roots in the spirit, so prayer becomes the mechanism that God uses for spiritual releases. (2019, 30)

It becomes imperative for our focus to remain on God during times of evaluation—especially if our motives behind genuine service to God are questioned by others. Bishop Paul S. Morton expresses the importance of focusing on God in his book *Changing Forward*. He states, "There will always be people who suspect your motives. To change forward you have to keep your eyes on the Lord, and prayerfully do what is pleasing to Him." (2012, 76).

Passion in Prayer—Unlock Alignment

The fact that motives can be deceptive is the real issue. Someone can do what seems kind, but their intentions may be completely immoral. Similarly, acting or completing a deed because you have something to prove nullifies the purity of the deed preformed. Those with nothing to prove are more impactful in their actions. The impact is evident because they are accomplishing out of passion, rather than competition or hopes of esteeming self.

When it comes to managing unhealthy competition, let's ponder it from a marathoner's perspective. Those involved in marathons usually do so for some form of personal development or goal. They may run in the same race, but focused athletes understand they are not motivated by the need to compete against others. They embrace the perspective of running their own race. By doing so, alignment with a pure motive within self is unlocked.

In some instances of life, we can agree, competition is healthy to a certain extent. But it is only healthy up to the extent which pride begins to set in and take dominion over our actions. Therefore, since competition is rooted in unhealthy pride, one can conclude there is no such thing as healthy competition in the Kingdom. In the Body of Christ there is absolutely no room for the smallest measure of unhealthy pride. Scripture informs us, in Galatians 6:4, there is a healthy measure of pride in evaluating self, but when it spills over into comparing yourself to others it becomes unhealthy. The Bible says, "Each one should test their own actions. Then they can take pride in themselves alone, without comparing themselves to someone else" (NIV).

Properly managing unhealthy competition is integral to keeping motives pure and living an impactful life. The grace to manage unhealthy competition is released through prayer. Similarly, the grace to live an impactful life is released through prayer. If you want to be impactful, then ask God to ignite your passion. Passion (or fervency) in prayer is a catalyst to bring forth change. The Bible says in James 5:16, "[T]he effectual fervent prayer of a righteous man avails much." The New American Standard Bible (NASB) says it "accomplishes much." A true measure of impact in prayer is directly related to the amount of change it generates.

The Pursuit of Prayer: Character and Integrity

Establishing a means of self-evaluation is about maintaining character and integrity as you pursue success. As mentioned in chapter 1, God wants you to accomplish and prosper. He anoints you to achieve the desires of your heart according to His will. Part of achieving the goal(s) we desire is found in a resolve to protect our character and integrity—purpose in your heart to be intentional about protecting your integrity. Character and integrity determine the level of your anointing. Jesus alluded to this in Mark 8:27 and Matthew 16:13. He asked His disciples, "Who do men say that I am?" In essence, Jesus took a census of His public character and integrity. This suggests He understood elevation without integrity and character is meaningless. Your authority and ability to influence is hindered if you are in leadership capacity and refuse to protect your character and integrity.

Although subordinates and peers may adhere to our input, being leaders of questionable integrity damages God's intended purpose for our lives. In the same manner, being a leader of integrity carries a greater dimension of influence and respect. This is vital to embrace. The alignment of your integrity and God's purpose, occurs through diligence in prayer. As mentioned in chapter 2, an inability to serve in the midst of opposition is detrimental to elevation. Similarly, an impure motive in pursuit of prosperity or success is damaging to one's ability to walk in integrity and character. Motive can be a qualifier, or it can be the means by which you are disqualified contingent upon the intention(s) of the heart.

A servant cannot afford to have a "what's-in-it-for-me" mentality; if they do, their service is in vain. The purity of servanthood is maintained when God's agenda rules the motive of our service. Having the wrong motive behind serving others, can negatively impact future pathways to success. To keep God's agenda at the forefront of your success, motives must be evaluated regularly. It becomes vital to evaluate and assess your approach and heart's posture. The evaluation process is cultivated through time in prayer and the ability to abide in His Word. The impact behind the motive for sowing a seed is revealed upon release of the seed. People always advocate for seeds to be sown into "fertile" ground, which is wise and biblical.

What exactly determines the fertility of the ground? Is it fertile when they can do something for me down the road? Is it fertile if we are keeping it in the family? The bottom line is when your motive is pure, fertility is measured by God's guidance and His wisdom. If God leads you to sow, it's fertile ground. It doesn't matter if the seed is sown into a homeless individual or an already established millionaire. To go *From the Bottom to the Top* you must sow out of obedience to God. Do not sow out of popular opinion, eloquent words, emotional ties, or the status of the one receiving.

I know it may sound crazy and unconventional, but it is okay to sow into someone or something that "cannot do anything for you." Colossians 3: 23–24 says, "[A]nd whatever you do, do it heartily, as to the Lord and not to men, knowing that from the Lord you will receive the reward of the inheritance; for you serve the Lord Christ" (NKJV). In other words, the essence and power of sowing abides in obedience and the essence and power of the harvest dwells in the motive.

No matter the size of the seed sown, it has the potential to unlock opportunities by way of the anointing, but do not make the mistake of believing the anointing can be purchased. If you are sowing time, money, or your talents, remember it's a service that's taking place unto God. Keep your motives pure as God accelerates you *From the Bottom to the Top* because motive truly does matter.

~*Motive Matters: An Issue of the Heart*
End-of-Chapter Prayer~

Lord, I ask that you cleanse me of any impure motives. Proverbs 16:2 reveals to me a person's ways may seem pure to them, but the Lord weighs our motives. I ask, in Jesus's Name, that You would weigh my motives. I open my heart to You for purification, according to Matthew 5:8, because my desire is to see You active in my life. Measure my motives according to your Word. In all that I do, I decree, my motive shall be to glorify You. I pray my motive will be driven by pure intentions for success and not an impure desire for promotion or any platform. I pray that whatever I do, I do it unto You and not for men according to Colossians 3:23. According to 1 John 1:9, I thank You for being faithful and just to forgive my sins and any impure motives I may have committed or operated in. I declare the anointing over my life to walk in the place of promise You ordained for me. I decree the strength to keep moving forward as I find strength in You according to Job 17:9. I pray You would empower me and uphold me in my integrity and set me in Your presence according to Psalm 41:12. I thank you for and I receive the anointing to walk in the integrity of the upright that guides, according to Proverbs 11:3. According to Lamentations 3:40, I pray you would endow me with the grace to examine my ways so that I can dwell in a place of purpose that is pleasing in Your sight. In Jesus's Name, Amen.

Journal the Journey . . .

_____

_____

_____

_____

_____

_____

_____

_____

_____

_____

_____

_____

_____

_____

_____

_____

_____

_____

_____

_____

Chapter 4

BUILDING YOUR MOMENTUM: GETTING GOING BY FAITH

"The ideal man bears the accidents of life with dignity and grace, making the best of circumstances."

—Aristotle

THE CONCEPT OF STANDING FIRM OR BUILDING momentum in your faith in the midst of opposition is not a simple task. There will be moments of doubts and feelings of weariness. Regardless of how you feel, you must stay the course. It's important to monitor your heart's response to life's situations. Proverbs 4:23 says, "Keep your heart with all diligence; for out of it are the issues of life" (NKJV). The New Living Translation of Proverbs 4:23 declares, "Guard your heart above all else, for it determines the course of your life." The heart is powerful because our feelings flow from it, which speaks to our response to the issues of life. Moreover, the heart is how we respond in faith.

We believe in our hearts (Romans 10:9). We trust with our hearts (Proverbs 3:5–6). Therefore, to build momentum in the area of our faith, we must place the Word of God in our hearts. In doing so, we position our hearts to respond in faith and carry the voice of faith. A voice of faith is cultivated in our prayer posture but begins in our meditation of scripture. Please note meditation is not memorization. I like to define memorization as simply committing to memory without revelatory comprehension. Meditation is the means by which we capture and comprehend the essence of scripture in our hearts.

Meditation of Prayer: A Heart that Speaks Faith

Meditation breeds faith and cultivates our hearts to respond in faith. It allows us to capture revelation and gain faith capacity in doing so. This is important to understand because your heart

47

speaks and has a voice. Jesus said in Matthew 12:34, "For out of the abundance of the heart the mouth speaks." This suggests the heart has a voice. The mouth is used, by the heart, to release what's in the heart into manifestation. Therefore, our hearts carry the ability to shape our reality and direct the course of your faith in God. This is why it's vital to keep the Word of God on our hearts. In doing so, our hearts can respond in faith instead of responding based on emotion. As our hearts respond in faith, our speech will become a speech of faith. Our declarations and decrees become faith centered. They ultimately impact our ability to pray and see the manifestation due to an enlarged faith capacity that began with our hearts.

The ability to get going by faith requires the heart and mouth to advance in agreement. Jesus is clear in Matthew 21:22: "[W] hatever things you ask in prayer, believing, you will receive." The issue is sometimes found in our inability to ask in faith. There are often occasions when our faith is hindered, or limited, by the residue of unbelief or doubt that may be in our hearts. This is why prayer becomes so important during seasons of opposition. We cannot allow feelings of depression, insecurities, or sorrow to hit our lives to the point of impact to our prayer life.

To build momentum on your journey to the top, you must resolve to press pass emotional warfare and trust God! In our lowest and weakest moments, we need the willpower to pursue His presence through intentional and fervent prayer. During those prayer encounters, God will release the grace we need to get going by faith. This is why He told the Apostle Paul, in 2 Corinthians 12:9, "My grace is sufficient for you, for My strength is made perfect in weakness." The grace released through the power of prayer will enlarge your faith and dismantle any self-perceived limitations.

Faith is not contingent upon our ability. A definition I often preach and teach as it relates to faith is faith is when our inability connects with God's ability. Matthew gives us insight in Matthew

26:36–39 of Jesus's pursuit of fulfilling His divine assignment while navigating human feelings of despair.

> Then Jesus went with them to a place called Gethsemane, and he said to his disciples, "Sit here, while I go over there and pray." And taking with him Peter and the two sons of Zebedee, he began to be sorrowful and troubled. Then he said to them, "My soul is very sorrowful, even to death; remain here, and watch with me." And going a little farther he fell on his face and prayed, saying, "My Father, if it be possible, let this cup pass from me; nevertheless, not as I will, but as you will."

The truth of the matter is the assignment or the plan of God for our lives will challenge the posture of faith we operate in. Therefore, the question becomes what do you do when the plan of God for your life begins to unfold but you are emotionally and sometimes psychologically uncomfortable during the process? When engaging in situations that challenge our faith posture, we must stand firm in faith through prayer and trust in the One that has anointed us! Proverbs 3:5–6, says, "Trust in the Lord with all your heart, and do not lean on your own understanding. In all your ways acknowledge him, and he will make straight your paths" (ESV).

The Message Bible's version of Proverbs 3:5–6 highlights the importance of listening for God's voice. The scripture says, "Trust God from the bottom of your heart; don't try to figure out everything on your own. Listen for God's voice in everything you do, everywhere you go; he's the one who will keep you on track" (MSG).

Ears to Hear—Intentionally Positioned to Listen

Listening or the ability to hear is a vital component to prayer and intercession. Knowing and learning to listen for the voice of

God are key to receiving instructions, guidance, and an increase to the measure of faith. Romans 10:17 informs us that "faith comes by hearing, and hearing by the word of God." This suggests the formula for accuracy of hearing requires revelation knowledge of His Word. Building momentum requires a resolve to become intentional about hearing the voice of God. Ask God to remove any hindrances to your ability to listen and recognize His voice. Ask Him in prayer to quiet the noise of life and open your heart to His voice.

If stagnation is present in your ability to hear from God for any given time period, then there is probably a hindrance to His voice. It may also be accompanied by an absence of His direction. God is always speaking and giving instructions to us by His Spirit. God's consistency in speaking does not change toward us. In Jeremiah 33:3, God says, "Call to me and I will answer you, and will tell you great and hidden thigs that you have not known" (ESV). The issue is not God's speaking; it is our ability to be in position to listen.

Our consistency in listening should change for the better during seasons of opposition. Meaning, we listen attentively while navigating through difficulty. A word of confirmation from God should breed action in the life of a believer. Therefore, it's critical to understand the importance of prayer and meditation. They both play a vital role in your journey to the top. Prayer and meditation are pivotal in your spiritual development and maturation.

To further your momentum, you cannot afford to succumb to distractions or adhere to instructions from strange voices. On the journey to the top, we must purpose to be intentional in guarding against internal desires of self-aggrandizement and external distractions. In his book *Momentum for Life*, Michael Slaughter shares a revelation on navigating the lure of strange voices. He says, "As you ascend the road of God's calling, the voices grow louder in their attempts to lure you to promises of self-gratification."

Jesus alluded to the urgency of avoiding the strangers voice in John 10:5. The Jesus conveys, "Yet they will by no means follow a stranger, but will flee from him, for they do not know the voice of strangers." He also declares in John 10:27, "My sheep listen to my voice; I know them, and they follow me" (NLT). The aforementioned verses of scripture are crucial to living by faith. Both verses reveal we must remain connected to the Source of our faith through communion with God. The verses also suggest our ability to listen to His voice has a direct relation to our ability to follow God. Moreover, our ability to hear is important since it is through the ability to hear we receive instructions, guidance, and revelation.

This may come as a surprise, but the anointing on your life is not meant to operate in comfortable situations. Similarly, the grace God gives us is not meant for us to accomplish things we can do on our own. It is given to us to accomplish what we cannot achieve on our own. The Apostle Paul alludes to this in 2 Corinthians 12:9, as God spoke to him about the manifold nature of His grace. The scripture reveals that God's "grace is sufficient for you, for my power is made perfect in weakness."

We need Him to share His plan with us and give us grace to endure the difficult seasons. God always has a plan that supersedes our ability to fabricate a resolution to a problem. This is why we need to remain postured as a people of prayer and embrace the power of listening. The ability to actively listen for His voice gives us direction of purpose and insight to potential.

God has a plan and is the author and finisher of your faith according to Jeremiah 29:11 and Hebrews 12:2. Who better to receive instructions from? In Jeremiah 29:11, we see this affirmed. The Bible says, "'For I know the plans I have for you,' declares the Lord, 'plans to prosper you and not to harm you, plans to give you hope and a future'" (NIV). The word *plan* in Hebrew is *machashabah*. It translates plan, thought, or purpose. It speaks to God's Sovereignty over the life of His creation. In the midst of giving hope and increasing our faith, through prayer, God releases instructions and His thoughts to us. Through prayer, as we listen, understanding and knowledge of our purpose is given.

The Confession of Prayer—Trust His Faithfulness

Gaining momentum in the area of faith urges us to hear and respond in obedience. It is not our responsibility to make anyone embrace your God inclinations or what you hear, but it is our responsibility to respond instantly through obedience to God. The obedient response unlocks perseverance. When perseverance becomes your dwelling place, your confession of faith grows. You begin to recognize and embrace His consistency as Deliverer, Provider, and Protector. The writer of the book of Hebrews says in Chapter 10, verse 23, "Let us hold fast the confession of our faith without wavering, for He who promised is faithful" (NKJV).

In other words, your memory of God's faithfulness is a direct reflection of what you confess about Him. If you remember Him as Healer, you will have no problem confessing Him as Healer. If you remember Him as Provider, you will have no problem confessing Him as Provider. The faithfulness of God and His consistency will speak through you no matter how bad things seem to be. This is why the scripture declares, in Hebrews 13:8, "Jesus Christ is the same yesterday and today and forever" (ESV). Get going by faith, that if He did it for you last time your back was against the wall, He can bring you out this time. Choose to respond in faith!

The Apostle Paul told the church in Corinth to "[b]e watchful, stand firm in the faith" (1 Corinthians 16:13 ESV). In chapter 2 we discussed the importance of perseverance. Perseverance is a key component of ensuring you stand firm in the faith and gain momentum. It is directly related to our ability to trust in God. To thrive in the midst of opposition, you must realize the process is linked to your ability to persevere, and your perseverance is identified by your ability to trust God. Instead of focusing on your natural inability, focus your faith toward God's enabling ability to work through you. The writer of the book of Hebrews beckons us to greater levels of faith and focus in chapter 12, verse 2, by saying, "Looking unto Jesus, the author and finisher of our faith . . . ."

The ability to trust the promise He made you and His leading must remain at the forefront of your perspective to counter every negative thing that comes your way. He designed a path uniquely tailored for you.

> The path created for you is just as unique as the destiny and success God has ordained for you to achieve. Trust God's leading!

Standing firm in your faith declares to the world, "I want all that God has for me!" Along with informing the world, you prove to God your desire to obtain the promise. The aforementioned acts are what I like to refer to as having evident faith, meaning the faith others can see or will eventually see. Please allow me to explain.

Immediately after you read the previous sentence, I'm sure you had questions. Several Bible verses probably came to mind that seem to contradict my previous point. Scriptures such as "[f]or we walk by faith and not by sight" (2 Cor 5:7) would probably be at the top of the list. Let me bring some clarity to the fact that others can see or will eventually see your faith. This would best be explained by taking a look at the "Hebrew Hall of Faith," as Hebrews 11 is commonly referred to. It lists a series of patriarchs who overcame obscurity and opposition because of their ability to stand firm in their faith. The chapter opens up with the words, "Now faith is the substance of things hoped for, the evidence of things not seen" (Hebrews 11:1 NKJV).

A deeper study of this verse reveals the concept of evident faith. Evident faith is the catalyst that takes our blessings that are stored up in the spirit realm and manifests them in the natural. In the midst of uncertainty, evident faith will cause you to triumph. The word *faith* in Hebrews 11:1 is the Greek word *pistis* which means "to have conviction of the truth" or "to have belief of divine things." The word *substance* in the text is the Greek word *hypostasis,* which means a setting or placing under which has foundation or is firm. In other words, Hebrews 11:1 reveals, "Now [divine belief] is the [foundation] of things hoped for . . . ."

Viewing the scripture from this lens suggests the proof and patience of a Christian's faith, which is planted in the Word of God, is the foundation for which manifestations can take place. To help clarify what may seem to be a complex thought; enduring the trial by standing firm in faith, will yield results. In order to stand firm in faith, we must examine what we believe and align our divine belief, which is our faith, with the Word of God. By aligning our faith with the Word of God, we can prevent spiritual collapses that are caused by the pressures of this life. The best reaction to pressure is performance.

The performance I am alluding to speaks of practical alignment of your faith with scripture. Doing so limits the potential to fall in the midst of opposition, and it fortifies your ability to stand firm. The Apostle Paul wrote in 2 Timothy 2:19, "[T]he foundation of God standeth sure" (KJV). This suggests God has the ability to stabilize those that trust in Him. He can stabilize us emotionally, socially, economically, or financially. There is a twofold task when standing firm in faith and building momentum. First, we must trust Him. Secondly, we must speak what He has spoken.

In his book *Beyond Personal Power,* Bishop Clarence E. McClendon gives his biblically based definition of having a "God-kind of Faith." He says, "The God-kind of Faith speaks what it believes, or what it wants to happen, based on the Word of God." (2003, 15). God has nothing but positive things to speak concerning your future! I have resolved in life and dare to suggest the discipline of God is tandem or directly in relation to our obedience, which we will discuss in later chapters throughout the book. I am not referring to moments of falling short. In those moments, we depend and rest in the hope and grace of God.

I am, however, referring to willfully and consistently being disobedient or undisciplined in the things of God. That type of inconsistency can be a disturbing hindrance to your ability to obtain all God has for you. For now, just resolve that the main thing standing between you and what you desire for God to do in you and on your behalf is your ability to remain disciplined. As a result, you must make up in your mind to prepare for the blessing. You must resolve to discipline yourself in preparation for your destiny. The more you walk in discipline, the more you will walk in obedience, ultimately impacting your faith in a positive manner.

The Hope of Prayer—Faith that Supersedes

As it relates to your future and your purpose, as mentioned in chapter 1, God has "plans to take care of you, not abandon you, plans to give you the future you hope for" (Jeremiah 29:11). The ability to possess the future you hope for is found in your ability to exercise the "God-kind of faith" that breeds "evident faith." Regardless of all the things people said about you in the past, what they are saying about you presently, or what they say about your future, your faith can supersede (take authority over and render useless) any persecution or ridicule you are facing or may have faced. Some people are okay with you having faith but start acting differently toward you the moment you show the slightest confidence in God by calling it pride. Don't be fooled by a controlling spirit—it's only pride if your faith does not point back to God.

As you submit to the foundation of Jesus Christ being planted in your life and as you press through the proofing of your faith, which will birth patience, God will bring forth the manifestation and make your faith evident to others. Evident faith will always bring forth a manifestation. Therefore, you must view opposition as beneficial. Although it may not feel like it, it is a tool of preparation for the promise. After your faith is tried, God will reveal your faith as evident.

Several examples of this biblical principle can be found all throughout the Bible. Some of them are specifically listed in Hebrews 11. Hebrews 11:4 says, "By faith Abel offered to God a more excellent sacrifice than Cain." The manifestation: "[H]e (Abel) obtained witness that he was righteous" and "God testified of his gifts." "By faith" Enoch's ways pleased God. The manifestation: "[H]e did not see death" (Hebrews 11:5). The Bible says, "By faith Noah prepared the ark." The manifestation: "God saved his household" (Hebrews 11:7). The Bible says in Hebrews 11:11, "[S]he (Sarah) judged Him faithful who had promised." The manifestation: "God allowed her to conceive."

Jesus alluded to this principle of faith being evident by the results it yields in John 10:37. He said, "If I do not do the works of My Father, do not believe Me" (NKJV). In John 14:11, Jesus said, "Believe me that I am in the Father and the Father is in me, or else believe on account of the works themselves" (ESV). In essence, Jesus said, since I am teaching and preaching faith in God and yielding results, have faith in Me. By no means is the gospel message one of receiving only. It is a message of hope and faith in Christ. An often-forgotten reality of hope and faith is results. Through prayer and intercession, your faith will yield results!

Build momentum in faith through prayer and meditation. Faith gives us the momentum to keep going. Believe by faith that God has you and your situation covered. Receive the fact that God shall perfect and complete all things concerning you! That which was held up or denied to you shall be released as your faith engages His presence through prayer. What you delayed in accomplishing, Heaven is backing with Divine momentum to complete it through fervent intercession.

The Evidence of Prayer—Manifested Harvest

The principle of evident faith is also found in Mark 16:17. Jesus said, *"[A]nd these signs shall follow them that believe."* This lets us know the faith of a believer can produce tangible manifestations. Although the verse specifically discusses casting out demons, speaking in new tongues, picking up serpents, drinking deadly poison, and laying hands on the sick, at its core, it is a verse focused on the concept of faith yielding results.

The end state of the previously mentioned list is obviously not a list of things we should go out and do intentionally—by no means. The end result and revelation to embrace is "it will not hurt" you if accomplished with the right degree (or measure) of faith (Mark 16:18). This is simply alluding to the fact that faith should eventually yield a manifested harvest. As a result, when you are standing firm in your faith, remember not to complain. Complaining throughout your test or trial takes away from your testimony. It has the potential to limit the results you achieve. Rather than complaining, choose to develop your prayer life in solitude. Learn to momentarily isolate yourself in prayer and intercession.

Prayer is a required skillset. It provides protection during the process. To achieve success and overcome in the midst of opposition, there has to be a tenacity to pray. You do not need to be the most eloquent or the lengthiest when it comes to prayer. Only believe! Jesus said in Mark 9:23, "If you can believe, all things are possible to him who believes." The Amplified Bible says, "Jesus said to him, "[You say to Me,] 'If You can?' All things are possible for the one who believes and trusts [in Me]!" The discipline to pray is cultivated by God as we align the belief in our hearts with His will.

Resolve to not wonder aimlessly in faith. Depend upon His leading and engage His presence. In her book *Compass: The Roadmap to Success*, Marcia Morrison proclaims the reality of a life without prayer and the benefit(s) a life of prayer yields. She states,

> A prayer-less life and ministry will propagate a clouded path and will cause one to wonder aimlessly in the wilderness. Prayer serves as a sure compass for your journey, no matter how dark the night or how cloudy the day. (2008, 26)

Effective prayer is based on the posture of the heart and the fervency of faith. Obtaining success and elevation through prayer is not about the longevity of prayer; it's about our heart's posture in Christ. It will prove nearly impossible to build momentum in your faith without prayer. Moreover, it will become extremely difficult to pray and not pray from a pure posture. Purity in heart involves having the right motive and desires behind what we pray. Purity is not about perfection; it's about focusing on being purposeful. Consistency in relationship and fellowship with Jesus Christ drives our purity of motive and directly impacts our response to purpose. It also determines the response we release in the midst of opposition.

Isolation in Prayer—Consecrated in Purpose

There are some things in your life only having faith in God will accomplish. Relying on the wrong people (and on those who we view as the right people) can dilute the strength of God in you. Throughout your journey, the relationship you work to form with God will cause you to look to Him for guidance and fellowship. It will unction you to rest in Him during seasons of opposition. Thus, purity will be established. When purity is established, prosperity is released and begins to flow unrestricted.

Psalm 1:1–3 reassures us of this principle of Godly prosperity. The scripture says,

Blessed is the man Who walks not in the counsel of the ungodly, Nor stands in the path of sinners, Nor sits in the seat of the scornful; But his delight is in the law of the Lord, And in His law he meditates day and night. He shall be like a tree Planted by the rivers of water, That brings forth its fruit in its season, Whose leaf also shall not wither; And whatever he does shall prosper.

When navigating opposition, purity will call for seasons of isolation. In a very social society, we tend to minimize the need to be isolated. Why do you think the scriptures record Christ going "away" to pray? (See Luke 5:16) Truthfully, He could have prayed in the midst of others, but His going away to pray informs us there is power in isolation. Ken Blanchard and Phil Hodges expound on the powerful realty of isolation/solitude in their book *The Servant Leader*. They explain,

Solitude and silence give us some space to reform our innermost attitudes toward people and events. They take the world off our shoulders for a time and interrupt our habit of constantly managing things, of being in control or thinking we are. (2003, 88).

Learning to be "okay" with isolation is part of the price we must pay to walk in a realm of greater grace and glory. It is a necessary part of engaging the process of success and spiritual growth. Solidifying our ability to stand firm in the faith requires it. By no means am I suggesting that you neglect to honor the word of the Lord in Hebrews 10:25. The scripture is clear: "and let us not neglect our meeting together, as some people do, but encourage one another, especially now that the day of his return is drawing near" (NLT). I am passionately conveying the direct relationship momentary isolation produces as it relates to obtaining strength to carry out your assignment. It is a means of rejuvenation. Some may even call it consecration.

Consecration carries a deeper and more strategic purpose in my opinion. Consecration is an intentional separation or setting apart for an intended purpose. Isolation is similar, as it relates to setting apart, but it carries a protective purpose of the one or thing that is being set apart. Therefore, I am speaking of daily moments of isolation to recharge your faith regularly and protect you from the issues of life. Isolation ushers us into a place of renewal, refocus, and rededication to our purpose. At times, spiritual isolation is necessary for effective consecration. When you find yourself in this type of isolation, it is usually for one of two reasons. God is either working on you, or He is working in you to impact those you'll encounter in life.

Standing firm in the faith to build momentum is about simply resolving in your heart and mind to remain true to the process God has ordained for your life. Contrary to popular belief, it takes work; it won't just happen. Truthfully, any task worth doing takes work. If you are reading this book, then I believe you are a person of vision desiring more. There are two things linking your current situation to your manifestation: faith and promise. Do not lose sight of either one. The place most people and organizations fail is they have vision and a plan but lack the commitment and work ethic. They lack the ability to pursue and implement the necessary change(s) needed to succeed. A person of vision can't afford to be lazy. Laziness kills vision and causes you to abort destiny.

The rise *From the Bottom to the Top* demands a fortified level of commitment. It's about trusting the uniqueness in the process God designed for you and trusting the God of the process. It's perfectly okay if people do not want to see you successful. Resolve in your heart that you will not give up on a future of blessings due to hindering opinions. The process can be painful, but you must recall it carries a purpose. Do not view it as punishment; rather, view it as propelling potential. Keep standing firm in the faith.

Your destiny is waiting, and the development to handle it occurs in seasons of opposition. Do not give up! The very thing you are experiencing is making you impactful and building the momentum you need in faith for the journey to the top. Build momentum through your ability to believe and endure.

~*Momentum: Getting Going by Faith End-of-Chapter Prayer*~

Lord I thank you for the power to live by faith. I decree my faith in You is stable and steadfast. I receive the grace to stand firm in the faith and be courageous according to 1 Corinthians 16:13. I decree that my heart is encouraged, and I know my labor is not in vain according to 1 Corinthians 15:58. I receive the grace and power to fight the good fight of faith (1 Timothy 6:12). I thank you for the promise in Philippians 4:13: I can do all things through Christ who strengthens me. I pray your power will work in me as You do exceedingly and abundantly above all I can ask or think, according to Ephesians 3:20. I declare, You are releasing the grace to operate in signs, wonders, and miracles through the power of the Holy Spirit according to Romans 15:19. I thank You that my faith is not stagnant and unproductive. I decree my works are committed to You and my plans are established by You according to Proverbs 16:3. I decree it is evident and manifesting tangible results. I declare momentum in the area of my faith. I decree my faith is arising, and I shall not dwell in mustard seed faith, but I shall speak to mountains and not doubt in my heart, according to Mark 11:23. In Jesus's Name, Amen.

Journal the Journey...

_____

_____

_____

_____

_____

_____

_____

_____

_____

_____

_____

_____

_____

_____

_____

_____

_____

_____

_____

_____

_____

_____

Chapter 5
JOURNEY IN STRENGTH: FAITH NECESSITY

"Great spirits have always encountered violent opposition from mediocre minds."

–Albert Einstein

AS YOU'VE PROBABLY GATHERED BY NOW, ANY form of progress will likely be met with opposition as you journey to the top. This chapter focuses our attention toward what I like to call "hard truths" in the area of faith. Hard truths convey the process to elevation involves warfare. This truth is not meant for us to walk in paranoia; instead, it beckons us to walk in awareness. It requires that we remain attentive to our faith. It suggests faith becomes a necessity. On the journey to the top, faith in God is an imperative requirement due to opposition.

For example, once you accept the call to serve God from a pure posture, some individuals may begin to see God's anointing on your life. Some will view the grace He's given you to accomplish His will as a benefit to the kingdom of God. Others will view the grace God has given you from a lens of envy. Not only will they begin to see the achievements, but their envy may begin to grow, causing a potential for intense jealously.

There is a faith necessity that must accompany you in an environment of covert jealously. This is not a chapter of complaining or bleeding but rather one of communication. The intent is to communicate an often-overlooked reality of opposition. The reality is there are times when opposition will come from those close to us and from those we least expect. We will engage this more in chapter 7 as we disclose truths about warfare. Regardless of the source of opposition, resolve to journey in strength and accept that standing firm in faith is a necessity. Faith is a necessity because it provides you leverage.

Leveraged Faith—The Perspective of Strength

Leveraging the measure of faith to remain strong in disappointment and moments of betrayal is vital. Jesus and Joseph leveraged their faith in the most difficult of situations. The lives of Joseph and Jesus when studied involve their encounters with what seemed to be detours, distractions, and difficulty. The ability to leverage the measure of faith is alluded to in Romans 12:3. The scripture declares, "[T]hink with sober judgement, each according to the measure of faith that God has assigned" (ESV). This suggests believers should use the measure of faith God gave us as a foundation to gain the advantage in all circumstances.

The previous chapter looked at releasing the hurt from opposition. This chapter speaks toward the benefits encompassed in trials and how they ultimately serve a greater purpose in strengthening our faith. I've learned that during moments of rejection by people, God can reposition you in the spirit.

> The most painful event in life, if viewed from the lens of purpose, can yield the most positive results.

This is exactly what happened when Jesus was in the Garden of Gethsemane.

Initially, when He prayed to God the Father, He prayed the "cup" would pass from Him. Once His perspective changed as it related to the purpose of the persecution and the process, it immediately triggered a shift in His prayer. He then prayed, "[N]evertheless, Your (the Father's) will be done." This reveals that obstacles are a catalyst to the anointing God places on each believer. To say you do not want the obstacle is to say you do not want to embrace being anointed past your current placement in the anointing. Avoiding the opposition of the process suggests a refusal to grow in the spirit and in faith.

This concept is made known during Jesus's prayer in the garden. Praying, "[N]evertheless, Your will be done," suggests Jesus realized forfeiting the cross would equate to forfeiting the crown and His position at the right hand of the Father but most importantly His redemptive work as the Savior of mankind. It is critical to understand that persecution occurs when your purpose is in the process of development. Be patient by working through the process in faith. Work through the process by remaining diligent in prayer. Once you accept the need to shift your perspective, you will navigate the storms of the process more effectively.

Consistency in prayer is the breeding ground for acceptance of the shift in perspective. God does not obligate us to any one thing. He obligates us to a kingdom assignment and purpose; therefore, retaining the right perspective during the trial is critical to achieving all God has ordained for you. Perspective is key. The loss of perspective can be detrimental. In his book *No Limits*, John C. Maxwell states, "Our perspective is not determined by what we see. It's determined by how we see, and that comes from who we are." (2017, 115). Prayer recalibrates our sight and reveals who God says we are. On the journey to the top, you cannot afford to get caught up in what others are doing or not doing. Don't even fix your eyes on the fact that some people are doing less; focus on the fact that there is more for you to do.

Protective Custody—The Posture of Impact

Make no mistake about it: your rise to the top will require the effective navigation of storms by faith. Tremendous seasons of tests and trials bring tremendous seasons of growth and maturity if navigated properly. During the trials, as you surrender to God, He will place you in spiritual protective custody.

Spiritual protective custody is a place of protection far out of your enemy's reach. It is a place where your faith acts as a catalyst to destiny. It is a place of strength and greater focus. It is a place comparable to the hedge that secured Job and his family. Satan referenced the hedge in a conversation with God:

> Have you not made a hedge around him, around his household, and around all that he has on every side? You have blessed the work of his hands, and his possessions have increased in the land. (Job 1:10 NKJV)

Spiritual protective custody also refers to the "holy place" of the Lord David spoke of in Psalms 24:3–5. It may sound crazy to say someone is protected while they are facing opposition, but we must embrace that trials carry purpose. The reality is God's protection is always with us. Deuteronomy 31:6 says, "He is the One who goes with you. He will not leave you nor forsake you" (NKJV).

The declaration of "nor forsake you" alludes to God's protection. There are seasons in life when God will keep you and your giftings a secret. Don't be alarmed when God desires to protect you by keeping you hidden for a period of time. Those particular seasons are usually moments of preparation. When it comes to the things of God, as it relates to your destiny, there is always a period of preparation that occurs before publication. The period of preparation doesn't always feel good to you, but it's good for you. Rest assured the gift of God in you was given with a purpose. Seek the Giver through prayer as you unwrap it.

God often hides us in order to minister to us and condition us to make our greatest impact. During the process, your faith will become a necessity. Dependency upon God will prove to be key. Use the time you are hidden by God as a time of consecration. It is during those seasons of consecration that God will begin to direct and speak to you about His plans and purpose for your life. I often use the term *burnout* to describe a situation where work is taking place but purpose is unknown. Burnout occurs in a particular area when you misplace (lose sight of) or misdirect (utilize inappropriately) energy God intended for use toward your purpose.

Being intentional with time leads to productivity and a position of active rest. Active rest is a place where you create and accomplish but are not suffering from fatigue or frustration. Engaging in negative behaviors is one of the strategies the enemy uses to drain us. For example, being productive in real life means you cannot afford to be petty on social media. Time is too valuable. Invested time often yields positive results. The productivity of your time will cause you to obtain rest and reassurance of purpose.

To emerge *From the Bottom to the Top*, you must become intentional with your God-given energy. This means anything you have strength to do must be done with purpose in order to bear fruit. Become intentional with your talents, treasures, and time. Properly placed intentions will drive your level of focus and cultivate clarity of purpose. Pastor Paula White once stated, "You are here for purpose not popularity." Although we understand purpose can lead to popularity, it should not be your motive behind success or seeking elevation.

Popularity is driven by an audience's response to what you do. The moment you stop doing or they lose interest, popularity is lost. Purpose is driven by the assignment God has wired you to complete. The greatest difference is that God's consistency toward our purpose creates sustainability. The pursuit of popularity is unstable and unsustainable after people change their minds.

Capacity in Conflict—Develop in Divine Opportunities

Once you fully grasp the concept of trials being tied to purpose, expansion will be on the horizon. To fully fathom and appreciate the aforementioned concept, there has to be a willingness to confront challenges. Confronting the challenges of life is a means of development. One cannot say they want development without some measure of conflict. A reality of adversity, opposition, and conflict is the embrace of warfare.

Every season of warfare is really a season of opportunity. Seasons of warfare present us with the opportunity to mature and not give up. In essence, warfare is an opportunity to see what our current faith capacity is, and it opens us up to expand that capacity. In other words, our faith capacity (our ability to believe God for what seems impossible) is enlarged through seasons of warfare and increases our spiritual capacity.

The intensity of the warfare you're facing is an indicator of God's intensions toward blessing you. This is why we must resolve to pray and not faint. The magnitude of the warfare is an indication of the breakthrough God has for you. When you obtain the breakthrough, people will show up in the thousands. Only the genuine ones will encourage you during the difficult moments in life. Some of those difficult moments will lead to success and further elevation, but you must remain encouraged throughout adversity.

There are instances where God will send divine opportunity amid opposition. That's why you cannot afford to give up. Even when it seems hopeless, you must continue to prepare for the opportunity. Preparation for divine opportunity is where your focus must remain. Focus is necessary in faith because Divine opportunities have the potential to shift your season and your faith's expectation.

Divine opportunities strengthen you and develop resilience during moments of intense trials. Divine opportunities are released to us through fervency of prayer and expectancy in faith. It is in prayer that God maintains our focus, imparts strength to our faith, and cultivates our heart's posture toward His will. A huge component of faith is having the tenacity to prepare for what God will do as a result of your faith. The bible says in James 2:17, "[A] lso faith by itself, if it does not have works, is dead" (ESV).

Expressly, we have a part to play in our development in order to reach the next level of ascension in Christ. To journey in strength, do not take people's disdain personally. Their behavior is a plot of the enemy to harden your heart. The Bible calls you blessed if you're pure in heart (Matthew 5:8); retain the blessing and focus on keeping your heart pure. God has a way of reminding us why He chose to place us in a certain situation or position of growth. I call it a position of growth because as I've alluded to throughout this book, your placement in opposition is simply an opportunity for maturity.

The Power of Placement—Identify the Purpose

The power of placement is one that's often overlooked. No matter the career field, if you're a gardener or an architect, proper placement can be the difference between life and death. Proper placement can be the difference between stability or a collapse. You cannot properly develop in a place of confinement. Confinement is the breeding ground of frustration.

Abram (later named Abraham) went to a place God would show him to posture himself for the promised inheritance (Genesis 12:1). Jonah needed to be in the right place to share the Word of the Lord (Jonah 1:2). The Prophet Samuel had to go to Jesse's house to anoint David as king (1 Samuel 16:1). The prodigal son had to return home to find restoration (Luke 15:11–32). Joseph was divinely placed in the palace in a position of authority to later provide for and save his family during a famine (Genesis 45:9–25). Lastly, Jesus became obedient unto death by embracing the cross to save a dying world and redeem us back to God (Philippians 2:8; John 19:17; Mark 15:22).

All the aforementioned instances of proper placement are proof of the power it holds in our journey to the top. In every instance, each person faced some form of opposition, but their ability to journey in strength (even in their weakest moments) proved to be a tool of advancement. Faith in God during the process is imperative to journey in strength. Strength is achieved through His distribution of grace—grace to not only save us eternally but to complete the assignment of manifesting His purpose for our lives. His grace is sufficient to fortify our faith during our weakest moments. God told Paul in 2 Corinthians 12:9, "My grace is sufficient for you, for my power is made perfect in weakness" (ESV).

One of our faith tasks in the midst of opposition is to remain attentive to the opportunities hidden within our current situations, meaning during seasons of opposition, identify the purpose rather than the pain. Pursue God's intention and learn all the opposition has to offer. If you search the situation and remain emotionally unbiased, then you will encounter God's intent. In the midst of searching, God will provide strength for the process. His grace will prove to be sufficient for you. 2 Corinthians 12:9 is a scriptural base for our ability to journey in strength. The Lord told the Apostle Paul, "My grace is sufficient for you, for my power is made perfect in weakness" (NIV).

Joseph encountered God's intent for his life through dreams. I have heard it said that Joseph, in his immaturity, shared his dream prematurely. I understand the point behind the previously mentioned comment, but I'd like to convey a deeper point that requires our attention as we pursue to conquer opposition. First and foremost, we need to establish there is nowhere in the Bible, that I've found, where God honored the request of someone that spoke against or prayed against the God-ordained purpose of another individual. With that said, I do not fully agree that Joseph's issue was simply the verbal release of his dreams or visions. Although he did fail to exercise restraint in sharing his heart in regard to what God revealed to him, I believe there is a deeper systemic issue we need to be aware of.

I defend that Joseph was not necessarily naïve for sharing his dreams from a point some may call "youthful discretion." The deeper revelation announces He was naïve because he expected the hearers of his dreams to respond in a certain way due to their position(s) in his life. He expected praise but received persecution. He expected those with key titles in his life to be excited for him. This revelation brings us to an awareness we need to open our hearts to. The awareness is simply that we need to be mindful of our expectations of people regardless of the titles they hold in our lives.

It is vital to set prayer-derived expectations of relationships and organizations. The Bible conveys several instances of warnings about this throughout its pages. Someone being in your life and holding a title does not automatically suggest they are receptive to your Kingdom purpose. Their perception of his current placement caused them to misjudge God's ability concerning Joseph. They were focused on his now and literally could not see his next.

I recognize there are times people may not be ready to hear your dream and there are those that do not deserve to know what God is showing you, but the fact that you share it does not give them the power to kill a God-ordained dream. I also understand scripture declares in Matthew 6:3, "[D]o not let your left hand know what your right hand is doing," but the context of that verse primarily involves giving or any form of sowing in order to assist another person. There are those that have redirected its meaning toward secrecy of purpose and dreams.

Everything God places on your heart and in your spirit is supposed to be protected, but it is not intended for you to live in fear of disclosing. The Bible is clear: God has not given us a spirit of fear (2 Timothy 1:7). A portion of Joseph's mistake in handling the disclosure of his dreams was due to his ability to look internally (the familiar—family) for help that God already ordained to take place externally (the unfamiliar—Egypt). In other words, Joseph assumed his help would come from a comfortable and familiar source. Unbeknownst to him, God ordained the route to his place of prominence would come through the external, uncomfortable, and unfamiliar.

With that said, what is God leading you to do that seems to be uncomfortable and unfamiliar? Often, our moments of challenge will hold our greatest release of progress into the promise. Do not shy away from the unfamiliar. The scripture tells us in Matthew 4:1 that Jesus was led into the wilderness (an uncultivated region) to be tempted. The word *tempted* is the verb *peirazo,* which means "to try whether a thing can be done." It means to test for the purpose of ascertaining quality. This is very powerful because it suggests the unfamiliar and the uncultivated yield the potential to birth purpose. It alludes to the need to be tested because the test or opposition produces quality in our lives and matures us spiritually.

Remain Passionate—A Necessity of Purpose

The same reality Jesus faced on His journey to the top was present in Joseph's journey: the unfamiliar. At times, the unfamiliar is the gateway to the place of prosperity. Just as an unfamiliar wilderness served as a gateway for Jesus's ministry's affirmation and advancement, the unfamiliar environment of Potiphar's house served as a gateway for Joseph's ministry and prosperity. Although unfamiliar territories may yield the possibility of purpose, we must be mindful of the inherent opposition of the environment and realize the trial it presents serves a purpose. During the realization of the trial, faith in God becomes a necessity. It will become a necessity as people begin to deny you access on your journey. It will become a necessity even as internal insecurities and self-perceived limitations begin to surface.

People often misjudge the purpose of others due to their lack of status in an area. A misdiagnosis of purpose occurs due to a misguided view of destiny and is caused by hatred. They are not necessarily hating your dream. They simply hate the potential that your dream holds. This explains why individuals around you cannot comprehend your passion in certain areas: because they only see what's familiar. In most instances, they only see the past and present without looking at your potential wrapped in promise. I urge you to no longer live in fear about sharing your dreams. Share them with those that are willing to listen to your potential wrapped in promise. God has not given us a spirit of fear (2 Timothy 1:7), and neither does the Bible condone secrecy leading to deception. It urges us to move in wisdom.

Learn from Joseph's mistake. Speak to those who you discern will react in a Godly manner and celebrate with you. No one can kill a purpose or vision God has given life to. Dismiss the concept and ideology of "dream-killers" because God did not give you a dream that can die by anyone's hand but yours. That's right. Only you can destroy that which is inside of you. How can you kill your dream(s) and vision(s)? By failing to act upon them!

Every day you allow yourself to remain distracted, every moment your dream(s) are not prioritized or go on neglected slowly desensitizes you from fulfilling them. This occurs externally any time you associate with or place yourself in a contaminated environment. Desensitizing also occurs internally due to doubt, unbelief, or emotional turmoil. Cultivating a mindset of prayer and a pursuit of God's presence will keep you during moments of internal opposition.

God will always take you further than individuals think you deserve to go. To effectively journey in strength, do not allow self-perceived limitations to derail your thought life due to opposition. The principle of external opposition due to acceleration is held true in Joseph's life and in the life of Jesus. Joseph's family could not comprehend the plan of God for his life, and neither could the people that knew of Jesus's upbringing. They initially questioned, isn't this the carpenter, is this not Mary's son, and is His father not Joseph (Mark 6:3; Matthew 13:55; John 6:42)?

God intends for you to go far in life. Learn to rest in the plan He's developing in the midst of the trial, and position yourself for the place of prosperity. Embrace the fact that acceleration in success will breed hatred in the hearts of others but trust your blessings will be worth the process! Don't lose ground due to opposing forces. You must realize you cannot control their perception, but you can control your passion. Remain passionate about your destiny. The enemy understands what you shall be. His goal is to make sure you do not become all that God has predestined. Every day of your life, the goal should be to make the enemy out to be the liar Jesus proclaimed he is according to John 8:44.

The purpose behind the trial is greater than your now. Evidence of this is displayed through Joseph's life and is explained in Genesis 50:20–21. The Bible declares,

> But as for you, you meant evil against me; but God meant it for good, in order to bring it about as it is this day, to save many people alive. Now therefore, do not be afraid; I will provide for you and your little ones. (NKJV)

The aforementioned scripture is laced with evidence of Joseph's ability to remain focused in faith. To journey in strength, we must choose to shift our perspective off the problem and grab hold to the intent of God.

The fact that Joseph's trials ultimately positioned him to "save many people" and provide for his family clearly conveys the purpose behind the trial is greater than the plight. Therefore, keep working, believe, and keep pursuing despite the difficulty you encounter. Journey in strength! In doing so, your faith will remain active and engaged. Active faith cannot exist in an environment absent of a persistent work ethic. Keeping your faith active can shape your environment and your current situation. You may not be someone they want to know now, but when God gets through with you, you'll be someone they'll need to know later.

The fact that you are focused does not mean you feel you have arrived; it simply means you know that you are going somewhere and realize there is more in you. The purpose behind the test is normally revealed after the test is passed. Practically speaking, this is how answers to a question that may have escaped you during a test come back to your remembrance after the tension associated with a period of testing ends.

Visionary Focus—Live in the Grace to Accomplish

The life of Joseph teaches us several things about actively pursuing your vision. One of the most relevant lessons to be learned is vision will create opposition. If your vision does not create opposition, then it is simply a daydream. Impact is the obvious difference between a vision and a daydream. Visions yield results and birth change. Daydreams do not. They end when the dreamer snaps back into their current reality. Joseph's brothers mentioned their belief of his status as a "dreamer" and not a visionary in Genesis 37:19.

Although visionaries have dreams, they take them one step further by strategizing a pathway toward making an impact. Visionaries pursue the process to lead them into new territory. This occurs through actively engaged faith. Faith is a vital catalyst to carrying vision. A revelation to grasp is new territory brings new tests and new trials, but it also brings new grace to accomplish. You do not necessarily accomplish all you do because you want to; you accomplish it because you know what's at stake.

When you have a revelation of what's at stake, you learn the importance to developing your capacity and retaining a focus toward vision. Visionaries and those that desire to be successful understand individuals are not inherently required to believe in the visionary's capability (quality). Visionaries simply resolve to believe in their own ability (their capacity to do). In their ability (or capacity to do), the capability (quality) of the visionary will be revealed. Let me explain further. It's very possible for someone to be capable but lack the capacity or power to do what they are capable of. A simple definition I often use to define ability is ability is enacted capability. Ability speaks toward depth of competence in an activity leading to action.

The necessity to journey in faith requires capacity. Capability speaks towards potential without resulting in consistent productivity. One of my focused prayers for you as you read this book and navigate your way to the top is that God would grace you with the ability to prosper in all He allows you to put your hands and your thoughts toward despite opposition. Rest assured, the God-vision in you will live to bless those directly connected to you and others God has ordained for you to reach!

From one visionary to another, please don't limit the blessing of your vision to money. Praying to God for money is one thing, but praying to God for vision is something totally different. Vision is a legacy builder; it impacts generations to come if implemented according to God's will. Proverbs 29:18 says, "Where there is no vision, the people perish." Vision is a fiscal multiplier, and it speaks toward the development and maintenance of a legacy.

Understanding what's at stake provides you strength for the journey. Embracing the new in your life will cause you to embrace the grace to accomplish and build the legacy God intends for you to obtain. This is the hidden purpose within most trials. It empowers you with grace to accomplish as you intentionally remain focused. Dr. Cindy Trimm states in her book *Prevail*, "The mental attitude you hold toward your work or your aim has everything to do with what you accomplish." The ability to focus drives our diligence and our ability to accomplish. The ability to focus during opposition drives you toward destiny.

God in His Sovereignty provides us with a unique level of grace to deal with intense opposition. Our job is to focus on living in the grace He has afforded to us for each trail. Living in the grace afforded to us is the driving force that equips us for the next level, meaning once I pass this test in the grace given to me, I will be better prepared to handle the next level blessing(s) and any opposition that comes with it. The grace afforded to us requires our obedience. The unsaved are required to confess and believe (Romans 10:9–10). The biblical response to God's grace for the believer is obedience, too. Operating in the grace God provides serves as a pathway to maturity.

I understand the eternal salvation aspect of grace. I am more so speaking to the accomplishing factor of grace. The impact of operating in grace prompts a new level of spiritual growth, which yields evidence. Luke 2:52 speaks towards this grace. The scripture reveals, "Jesus grew in wisdom and in stature and in favor with God and all the people." Journey in strength by moving in faith. As you journey in strength through prayer, God will enlarge your faith capacity and release to you what's necessary to obtain the victory. 1 Chronicles 16:11 says, "Seek the Lord and his strength; seek his presence continually" (ESV). Continue to journey in strength on your way to the top.

~ Journey in Strength: Faith Necessity End-of-Chapter Prayer~

Lord, I thank You that you are the same yesterday, today, and forever according to Hebrews 13:8. I praise You for your consistency in being God, my deliverer, and being a God of sovereign intentions. I thank you, according to James 1:2–4, that the testing of my faith produces perseverance. I thank You that as a result of Your Word, every trial I encounter on my journey to the top is maturing me for your glory. According to Proverbs 3:5–6, I decree I am trusting You with all my heart and leaning not on my own understanding. I declare my faith in God is a necessity and rooted in Your Word. I decree Mark 11: 22 is my portion and I "have faith in God." My desire is to submit to You in all my ways that you may direct my path. I decree I am blessed because I persevere under trials and have stood the test according to James 1:12. According to Psalms 27:1, I declare you are my light and my salvation. I praise you because I have been graced to view every trial I face from the lens of purpose. I thank You, according to Jeremiah 29:11, that Your plan is to prosper me and not to harm me, in order to give me a future and hope. I receive the revelation of Luke 1:37: "For nothing will be impossible with God." I declare I shall be strengthened in faith for the journey according to Philippians 4:13 because I can do all things through Christ who strengthens me. In Jesus's Name, Amen.

Journal the Journey . . .

_____

_____

_____

_____

_____

_____

_____

_____

_____

_____

_____

_____

_____

_____

_____

_____

_____

_____

_____

_____

Chapter 6

DON'T SHOOT YOURSELF: FORGIVE

"We must develop and maintain the capacity to forgive. He who is devoid of the power to forgive is devoid of the power to love. There is some good in the worst of us and some evil in the best of us. When we discover this, we are less prone to hate our enemies."

—Martin Luther King Jr.

THE MOST DANGEROUS THING ANYONE CAN DO during a season of opposition is give up on their God purpose. Giving up is the gateway to committing spiritual suicide relative to success. Spiritual suicide is committed as opposition hinders you in the area of forgiveness. Do not inflict pain on your purpose by living with unforgiveness in your heart. Unforgiveness is a result of past or present hurt. Unforgiveness stems from the past, but pursuing deliverance from unforgiveness is a powerful catalyst to your future.

One of the most dangerous things about encountering hurt is its potential to impact your will to keep going. Hurt can come in various forms and stem from any source. It has the potential to throw anyone off course. It can make you bitter, rather than better. Do not allow affliction to cause you to see life from the lens of adversity. This explains the necessity behind the release to forgive. The ability to forgive yourself and others is cultivated in prayer.

Releasing Forgiveness—The Posture to Embrace Momentum

The release allows you to operate at the fullest level of God's anointing and purpose for your life. Releasing the hurt is a means to set free those who have hurt you. It has the power to grant access to all that God has for you. No matter who has hurt you or the nature of the situation, I declare over your heart a willingness to forgive and be healed. Releasing the hurt allows you to soar in the things of God.

Do not shoot yourself by dwelling in a place of unforgiveness. Forgiveness frees you from harboring negative feelings in your heart. The Bible says,

> Who shall ascend into the hill of the Lord? Who shall stand in His holy place? He that hath clean hands, and a pure heart; who hath not lifted up his soul unto vanity, nor sworn deceitfully. He shall receive the blessing from the Lord, and righteousness from the God of his salvation. (Psalm 24:3–5 NKJV)

Some individuals may inadvertently associate Psalm 24:3–5 solely with righteous living and being perfect. Righteous living is a factor in the text, but it does not call for perfection. This scripture primarily addresses the motive behind the actions of an individual. The portion that speaks to the importance of forgiveness is "clean hands, and a pure heart." Joseph and Jesus displayed this Kingdom principle to us in Genesis 50:20 and Luke 23:34.

Joseph made it known his brothers intended to harm him and meant evil against him, but God turned the situation around for his good (Genesis 50:20). Jesus prayed while on the cross, "Father, forgive them, for they do not know what they do" (Luke 23:34).

> Forgiveness is the essence of a pure heart.

Forgiveness qualifies you for ascension in prayer. The ability to forgive allows you to advance with momentum in life. Forgiveness frees you to operate within the heart of the Father. It dispenses the grace to be healed from betrayal and serve God at a greater level. Once you forgive, you posture your faith to trust again.

Often in life we find situations and issues will prompt us to either desire forgiveness, offer forgiveness, or grant forgiveness.

If we were to categorize any situation requiring the need for forgiveness, whether it be for ourselves or for others, then it would fall into one of the three previously stated areas. During the process of facing any situation, as you journey to the top, you will find the desire to forgive is usually the easiest of the three to operate in.

The "desire to forgive" simply says there is a part of me (and you) that recognizes there is something wrong that needs to be made right. It speaks toward the fact that we recognize an offense has occurred. The problem is neither party has accepted the responsibility to address the issue. The "offering of forgiveness" goes a step further. It surpasses recognizing something is wrong because during the offering process someone has accepted responsibility to address the issue. The problem with simply offering forgiveness is that it must be accepted, or it is rendered incomplete and thereby ineffective at its core.

By no means am I alluding to begging for someone's forgiveness. Neither am I suggesting you remain bound in spirit (or emotion) due to their decision to remain in an unrelenting position of anger toward you. The fact that some people will not forgive you of past mistakes rests in the reality that they are still dealing with some of their present insecurities. What I am saying is that forgiveness, at its core, takes the agreement of two individuals, similarly to how the offense requires the disagreement of two people.

Let's press a little further to gain clarity. The "granting of forgiveness" represents the core intent of the power to forgive. It is the most complex yet most rewarding of the three categories mentioned. It sparks not only the "desire to forgive" and the "offering of forgiveness," but it obligates and places demand on acceptance! In other words, granting forgiveness puts two once-opposing parties in a position of being in one accord.

Granting forgiveness unlocks the access needed to achieve. As a side note, if someone chooses not to forgive you, repentance to God will cover the offense and not hinder your progress to the top.

Being on one accord is vital to God's plan and His agenda for our lives, both naturally and spiritually.

Agreement in Prayer—Realignment with the Will of God

Throughout scripture we find God's will for us is to be in one accord. Matthew 18:19–20 records Jesus saying,

> Again I say to you that if two of you agree (one accord) on earth concerning anything that they ask, it will be done for them by My Father in heaven. For where two or three are gathered together (one accord) in My name, I am there in the midst of them.

Shortly after Jesus's statement on agreement, the parable of the unforgiving servant is told to Peter when he asks, "Lord, how often shall my brother sin against me, and I forgive him" (Matthew 18:21). This suggests a method of deliverance from an unforgiving heart is agreement, unity, or the ability to bring opposing forces into one accord through forgiveness.

Maintaining a forgiving heart ought to be the goal of every believer. Forgiveness speaks of our capacity to love as God loves. Surpassing the fact that it is the right thing to do, forgiveness grants the believer access to maximizing God's plan for their life. Luke 23:34 sheds light on this powerful concept. The Bible says, "Then Jesus said, 'Father, forgive them, for they do not know what they do.'" There are three things we need to notice about forgiveness through Jesus's first of His last seven sayings on the cross. After being mocked and beaten, having many blasphemous things spoken against Him, being lied on and accused of perverting others, treated with contempt, and the people insisting Pilate crucify Him, the scripture says, "Then Jesus said, 'Father, forgive them . . . .'"

The fact that "Jesus said" was an outward declaration of Christ's desire to remain aligned with God's will as it relates to

His salvation assignment for mankind. The intent is not to get engrossed with theology (the study of religious beliefs and theory) and Christology (the study of Christ), but Christ being 100 percent man and 100 percent God is the basis behind my previous comment. His God-nature was not the issue because it is in alignment with God's will.

The proclamation of forgiveness was directed toward the need to align His human-nature. Similarly, we should strive to forgive and align our human nature (or will) to the plan of God for our lives. The preliminary stage of Christ's salvation assignment and God's plan of salvation, as it relates to Calvary, is found in Christ's desire and ability to forgive.

In other words, God's plan to save us and forgive us hinged upon Christ's ability to forgive others. In other words, the proclamation of forgiveness reveals to God a desire to forgive. The blessing behind the confession of forgiveness is its birthing of a desire to forgive. The process of forgiveness begins in our confession. Once we speak our desire to forgive, God will adjust our attitudes, begin to shift our focus, and realign our perspectives.

Proclaiming forgiveness grants you access to transition from a victim's mentality to a victorious mentality. The proclamation of forgiveness says, "Although they hurt you, the pain you're experiencing has a Divine purpose." Although you may be going through something, as you make your journey to the top, the proclamation of forgiveness is a message of hope that it would be a mistake to count you out. The potential to forgive is one of persistency. The word *said* in the Greek is in the imperfect tense. That means Christ repeatedly or continuously prayed, "Father forgive them, for they do not know what they do."

Christ's declaration also informs us His persecutor's actions were completed from a place of ignorance. Forgiveness will help you to look past the ignorance of your accusers because you realize they do not perceive by any of their senses (neither do they have a full knowledge of) what they are doing. In other words, "Because they do not fully understand Who I am, and my purpose, they are doing wrong towards me from a lack of knowledge . . . so Father forgive them."

The reality is that on your journey to the top, there will be some people who will do wrong to you on purpose, but then there are those who will do wrong to you out of ignorance. The busy life you lead due to the level of responsibilities and goals you possess mandates you do not have residual time to figure out which category your haters fall into. Therefore, learn to pray, "Father forgive them," and keep moving.

The Pursuit of Forgiveness—Commanded in Purpose and Persistence

The fix to your dilemma is to move forward by resolving to forgive and release the hurt. The revelation behind the persistency of Christ's forgiveness, after all He had to endure, is found in the word *forgive* (Luke 23:34). To bring clarity, there are four moods for Greek words. Their purpose is to enlighten us as to whether the action is factual, potential, wishful, or a command.

The indicative mood gives designation as it relates to time (meaning past, present, and future). The subjunctive mood suggests probability or desirability. The optative mood suggests a wishful or potential statement. Lastly, the imperative mood indicates a command. The word *forgive* is in the imperative mood. This informs us that persistently forgiving is a command and not an option. The blessing behind the tense of the word *forgive*, as Jesus used it, suggests we must forgive without boundaries. Not only was Jesus fulfilling a command and having persistency in forgiveness to help us look past the ignorance of our accusers, but forgiving persistently helps us to forgive without limitations.

Luke 23:24 informs us of Christ's proclamation of forgiveness, His persistency of forgiveness, and lastly the power of forgiveness.

The word *forgive* in the text is *aphiemi*; in Greek, it means to send away or depart (to keep no longer). The blessing of *aphiemi* is not only found in the fact that you are letting go of something, but *aphiemi* also means to permit or allow. It means not to hinder, to leave and go away from, in order to go to another place. In other words, we need to be persistent in our forgiveness because forgiveness has the power to enable us to let go of something in order to gain something better!

Persistency in forgiveness gives us the power to let go of pain and pursue purpose. Jesus alluded to this power in Luke 22:69. The scripture says, "Hereafter, the son of man will sit on the right hand of the power of God." Christ is alluding to the fact that after I make it through all I am about to experience, not only will I complete my God-assignment, but I will gain my God-ordained position of authority and power. The same holds true for us. Once we overcome opposition, we gain our God-intended position of authority and power.

Enduring the process and coming out with a forgiving heart will grant you access in letting go of depression to gain peace. On your journey to the top, be persistent in forgiveness so you can receive the power to let go of hurt to gain healing. Forgiveness is the breeding ground for your breakthrough. Pursue forgiveness because it helps you to heal. Healing is important to your journey to the top. If you stay hurt too long, you can miss out on God-opportunities of advancement. If the possibility of advancement occurs without healing, then it is likely people will be hurt by you during the process.

There are numerous hindrances to forgiveness. There are several reasons why not to forgive the offense, but we must resolve and evolve in our understanding. Forgiveness is vital to your progress *From the Bottom to the Top*. We cannot afford to shoot ourselves with unforgiveness. No matter the reason, the inability to forgive can be traced back to immaturity at some level. Immaturity hinders the ability to forgive. This why we must desire to mature and not flee from the process of maturity. A desire for maturity helps tremendously as it relates to releasing the hurt.

The Choice of Forgiveness—Letting Go Leads to Deliverance

Sitting in my office one day, I received a revelation on forgiveness. It was an "open-eyed" vision of someone that seemed to be confined in chains, but they weren't. They were holding on to the chains themselves (had them wrapped around their wrist leading into their hands) and wouldn't let them go. The Lord shared with me there are times you must be willing to release the chains of pain, disappointments, and the hurt to be free. Let go. The chains aren't holding you; you're still holding them! You must choose to forgive your way out of the hurt and pain. No matter what may have happened to you, do not get so wrapped up in the pain of betrayal that you neglect God's intention of deliverance toward you.

Too often we lose sight of God's ability to deliver us, primarily for two reasons. The first reason is obvious: there is a measure of hurt that prevents our acceptance of deliverance. The second reason involves our level of comfort in membership. If you are comfortable in your church, then it's probably because you are in a position of membership rather than discipleship. Membership is comfortable, whereas discipleship is uncomfortable. Growth occurs in the midst of discipleship and not necessarily membership. Disciples ask questions. The questions are generated out of a propensity for growth and not out of a position of disobedience.

Evidence of this principle is proven in Luke 11:1 when the disciples said, "Lord, teach us to pray, as John also taught his disciples." One of the keys to success involves your ability to ask questions. Asking questions sparks creativity and the discipline to be attentive in your communication. Those that cannot appreciate your desire to ask questions are ultimately attempting to stifle your success and potential to grow.

Maturity in Prayer—Forgiveness Cultivates Discernment and Reveals Destiny

An important factor of growth is elevation. As you grow spiritually, you are positioned by God to achieve elevation in the natural and can expect elevation to take place in any area of your life. In other words, elevation cannot be achieved by membership; it must be achieved by discipleship. Elevation is an important factor of growth because it qualifies you for the place God desires to position you. The position of growth cannot be realized through an unforgiving or immature posture. Contrary to popular belief, although people may do so, God does not elevate the immature. Godly elevation finds you when your level of discipline surpasses your current title and collides with obedience. The hard truth is unforgiveness is a sign of spiritual immaturity, just as forgiveness is a sign of spiritual maturity.

To get past the hurt, you must understand God never called us to be emotionless and fake. He called us to forgive those that hurt us. It is okay to exhibit hurt and show signs of pain. The hurt you experience or show becomes an issue when you allow it to cloud your judgment. The other piece of caution is found in vulnerability. You cannot afford to be vulnerable around everyone. It's important to understand forgiveness grants us the ability to progress. Therefore, it becomes easy for some people to remain stagnant because they operate in an unforgiving spirit due to being hurt by others.

Hurt must never get in your heart because a hardened heart blocks the flow of God's promises into your life. It also hinders accelerated progress. A hardened heart contains malice, strife, anger, and a list of other emotions that are not of God. Jesus said,

"Blessed are the pure in heart, for they shall see God" (Matthew 5:8 NKJV). Do the best you can in life to retain a pure heart. Commit to praying and allowing God to show you the posture of your heart. Allow God to search your heart and inspect it daily. Do not fear the searching of your heart. It does not lead to God's punishment as some suggest; it ultimately leads to God's perfecting and His love. "For the Lord corrects those he loves, just as a father corrects a child in whom he delights" (Proverbs 3:12 NLT).

I vividly recall my pastor, Bishop Calvin Lockett, preaching a sermon on Matthew 5. I clearly remember one of the points he used to bring out the revelation of the focal scripture. He passionately closed his sermon by saying, "Not only shall you see God in Heaven, but you will see God active in your life on earth . . . so keep your heart pure." One of the keys to growth is learning to be grateful for every closed door you thought you were meant to walk through. In life, it's rewarding at times to understand that man's rejection is simply God's redirection. This can be applied to any relationship. There must be a clear understanding of redirection and rejection.

This becomes important to grasp because it is possible to be redirected by God versus being rejected by people. Dr. Cindy Trimm reveals this truth in her book *Push*. She states, "Rejection is a divine announcement that you were never supposed to prosper within a particular relationship or realm." The ability to properly discern and know the difference between being redirected by God and rejected by people is important to your destiny.

The Lord has a vested interest in your God-given assignment and destiny. Those that have ignored you will be required to pay close attention to you. The purpose God has for you will become indisputably evident. The clarity of your purpose comes to you through prayer and will be provided to others through the accomplishments God orchestrates throughout your life.

God does not reject those He is invested in. That's why you must go through the process of releasing the hurt and pray for increased discernment. Discernment helps you to embrace God's redirection. It allows us to also identify manipulation from people. This is especially important if God chooses to use people to carry out His redirecting. A distinguishing factor is God's redirection will not prompt issues with forgiveness; rejection from man will, meaning God's redirection settles in our spirits and does not leave any residue of emotional pain or unforgiveness. God gracefully redirects us to preserve us. Through consistency in prayer, we embrace His redirection, and it does not carry the weight of rejection we experience from people.

The reality is your progress in life will be met with many opportunities to choose forgiveness. It's not because difficult issues and experiences will not arise. It's more so about a choice to not give issues power over your life or your behavior. To effectively reign at the top, there must be a desire for God to reign in our hearts. Releasing the hurt is a self-medicating approach to receive healing from the spirit of rejection. It aligns your heart in a place of possibilities rather than a position of pain.

The place of possibilities is where the hurt can be released effectively. It's the place where God allows you to serve out of love toward what He has called you to instead of serving from a posture of pain. Choose to achieve by releasing the hurt. The release of unforgiveness will expedite your journey to the top! Pursue forgiveness and advance in God's purpose and plan for your life.

~ *Don't Shoot Yourself End-of-Chapter Prayer*~

Lord, I thank You for the grace to serve You with gladness according to Psalms 100:2. I pray a release from the hurt and wounds I received during my service to You and others. I break, rebuke, and cast out any spirits of hidden pain that would cause my heart to be hardened toward others. I receive the new heart and new spirit that you have promised according to Ezekiel 11:19 and 36:26. I declare my heart is receptive to Your will. I decree the ability to love and forgive at a greater dimension shall be my portion. I declare that all things I experienced have worked together for my good and for your glory according to Romans 8:28. I decree and declare I have a mind and heart to forgive anyone that has aggrieved me according to Colossians 3:13; I forgive them as You have forgiven me. I thank You; forgiveness is my portion and the fruit in my heart. I declare that I choose to forgive myself for past decisions and actions that did not bring you glory. I glorify You because all bitterness, wrath, and anger have been put away from me. I cast down all negative and ungodly emotions according to Ephesians 4:31. I thank you as a result of the grace to forgive; my journey to the top is not hindered, but it is progressive and gaining acceleration. I praise You for deliverance from past hurts. I thank You; I now have access to all You desire for me because I do not hold anything against anyone. In Jesus's Name, Amen.

Journal the Journey . . .

_____

_____

_____

_____

_____

_____

_____

_____

_____

_____

_____

_____

_____

_____

_____

_____

_____

_____

_____

Chapter 7

WARFARE: FRIEND OR FOE?

"Mountain tops inspire leaders, but valleys mature them."

–Winston Churchill

———————————

THE WORST KIND OF OPPOSITION IS THE ONE that is covert and often hidden. It is designed to make you feel as if you are the root of the problem. It is often released by a source you did not see coming. Some refer to this as friendly fire. Contrary to popular belief, measures of warfare are part of the assignment to success. Once you submit to embracing warfare, you ultimately are in a posture to receive the blessing. The term *friendly fire* is a military term used to explain harm or force imposed on someone by an ally. It suggests an unexpected attack from the most unlikely source. Sad to say, during your rise *From the Bottom to the Top,* not every opposition you face will originate from a known enemy.

During my early years of service in the military, a senior leader explained the concept of uniformity to me. I was told, "Uniforms are used to identify friends from foes." Let me explain why the aforementioned is a very powerful statement. In our everyday lives, there are people we interact with and confide in. There are those that support us and those that love us. The concept of uniformity is found in the fact that we have things in common with them. Uniformity speaks toward agreement and unity on some level. As a result, associations and relationships are formed. Whether we attend the same church, work together, have children that attend the same schools, and so on, the common factor or reality you share with them is normally the reason for uniformity.

War in Prayer—Engage and Grow

Relationships are formed at some level, and so are emotional ties and trust. The moment those relationships recognize the growth, advancement, or acceleration taking place in your life, the potential for friendly fire may arise. The most vital thing to understand about friendly fire is just that: it is disguised as being friendly. Friendly fire, at its core, is when the opposition you encounter comes from a familiar friend or associate. These are individuals who were once trusted allies but have chosen to make you their enemy for whatever reason—primarily due to envy, jealousy, or malice.

The journey to the top will breed friendly fire whether it is sibling rivalry, like what Joseph experienced, or a relationship you invested time and energy in, just as Jesus did with Judas. Friendly fire is a form of warfare. There are two unavoidable functions of warfare. They are, you must be willing to *grow through it*, and you must be willing to *engage in it*. Growing through warfare speaks to your tenacity and diligence.

Engaging in warfare speaks to your ability to receive strategy from God. Engaging in warfare can become detrimental if you fail to intentionally guard your mind (or will) through the vehicle of prayer. Succumbing to the pressures of life can impact our ability to fight and obtain the victory. Bishop Joseph Walker highlighted this revelation about the importance of time with God in prayer in his book *Reset Your Life*. He stated,

Jesus spent time alone with the Father no matter what the pressures on him. He would go into the mountains, setting aside time for prayer and meditation and for fasting. He knew his strength lay in his relationship with the Father, and those things nurtured that relationship. (Walker, 102)

A mind (or will) that is too strong can fall into pride. A mind (or will) that is too weak can fall into confusion and disorder, but a sound mind (or will) creates the opportunity for you to live life with a level of self-control that gives you power through Christ. This power allows you to love your enemies and overcome your fears and your insecurities. It is power that cultivates and releases strategy toward victory!

The Bible informs us in 2 Timothy 1:7, "For God has not given us a spirit of fear, but of power and love and of a sound mind." The English Standard Version of the bible says, "God gave us a spirit not of fear but of power and love and self-control" (ESV). In the midst of opposition, remember to walk in the aforementioned power.

The battle you are engaged in may feel physical, but it's a spiritual one. Ephesians 6:12, in The Amplified Bible, warns of this reality:

> For our struggle is not against flesh and blood [contending only with physical opponents], but against the rulers, against the powers, against the world forces of this [present] darkness, against the spiritual forces of wickedness in the heavenly (supernatural) places.

Keeping your mind fixed on God's plan for your life will prove highly beneficial as you engage in the mental and spiritual warfare associated with your journey *From the Bottom to the Top*.

Principle of Chapter 7—
Discernment is key to distinguishing friend from foe!

Discernment in Prayer—Try the Spirit during Acceleration

When it comes to friendly fire,

> Discernment is key to distinguishing friend from foe.

Be careful to develop discernment and not paranoia. Discernment is developed through the trials we experience. It is an indicator of our maturity. Hebrews 5:14 says, "But solid food is for the mature, for those who have their powers of discernment trained by constant practice to distinguish good from evil" (ESV). The reality of discernment is rooted in its Greek origin *diakrisis*. *Diakrisis* means to distinguish or judge.

This is vital when identifying friend from foe because it speaks to our ability to remain attentive and move strategically. We cannot fight effectively, if we are literally sleeping with the enemy. Nor can we judge accurately, if the enemy is feeding us intelligence. In the covert operations world, this is known as being a double agent. By definition, it is an agent who pretends to act as a spy for one country or organization while in fact acting on behalf of an enemy.

Some of us cannot effectively move in acceleration because we are trapped in a spy scenario with people we are tied to emotionally or socially but who have proven to be a hindrance to our progress in God. Our ability to move in deliverance begins with prayer. It begins by allowing God to reveal who they are. Once that is made known, the task of praying through the situation and cutting unhealthy soul ties becomes vital. There is a lot we can say about the process of deliverance. One thing we cannot fail to address is that identifying strongholds becomes key to obtaining the breakthrough. The reason some of us struggle to move in deliverance is because we are negligent in identifying the root issue.

In warfare, we must be willing to identify the enemy—even if the enemy is within us or those we call family. This may seem harsh to some because the essence of Christianity is love. While love is at the foundation of Christianity, God never called us to be manipulated or abused by anyone. The fullness of the gospel of Jesus is a balanced Gospel. We must evolve in our understanding of the Kingdom of God. Warfare is a key part of God's Kingdom and is a primary method of advancing it. Jesus said in Matthew 11:12, "From the days of John the Baptist until now the kingdom of heaven has suffered violence, and the violent take it by force" (ESV). The New Living Translation of Matthew 11:12 conveys, "[F]rom the time John the Baptist began preaching until now, the Kingdom of Heaven has been forcefully advancing, and violent people are attacking it."

A portion of your journey to the top involves warfare. This is why we covered forgiveness: because God wants us to extend love to our enemies through forgiveness. Even after identifying they are not for you, just as Jesus did with Judas, and Joseph did with those closest to him. Operating in the grace to guard against and relinquish limitations becomes critical to our ability to thrive during seasons of warfare. We must be willing to face the limitations placed on us by others and the ones we place on ourselves. The valley encounter exposes us to several truths; as we engage it through prayer and intercession. It will expose internal conflicts that exist within us. It will also expose external conflicts that exist in our environments and relationships.

In her book *Prevail*, Dr. Cindy Trimm speaks to the reality of opposition those called to accomplishing anything of significance will encounter. She states,

> If you are going to accomplish anything of significance, there are going to be times you will have to "sail against the wind" as you develop new skills. Such winds can blow externally or internally—driven by forces without as well as forces within. There are the naysayers, cultural constraints, the status quo, friends, family, competitors, and

the prevailing atmosphere or environment in which you live. Within, there are your own doubts, fears, insecurities, and emotions that can catch you by surprise and veer you off course. These forces must be harnessed and exploited to your benefit or you will find yourself shipwrecked. (Trimm, 118)

As we engage warfare and everything the enemy desires to send against us, we must comprehend the revelation John released in 1 John 4:4. The Bible says, "But you belong to God, my dear children. You have already won a victory over those people, because the Spirit who lives in you is greater than the spirit who lives in the world" (NLT). The Greater One is fighting with us and for us. No matter the internal warfare or the external warfare, our task is simply to *pray with fervency, discern in accuracy,* and *obey with urgency.* That is the formula to obtain Divine strategy and operate in the grace to overcome. Just as it was with Joseph and Jesus, no weapon formed against your purpose in God will prosper. His plan is perfect concerning you, and no one can hinder it. Our victory is sealed in Christ—not just in eternity but also here on earth. The process of advancement and acceleration is required to mature us and reveal to us the fullness of God's grace and capacity within us. We have dominion.

The ability to discern is the believer's portion. Some individuals have a hard time understanding discernment means to judge because they assume it is judgment leading to condemnation. That is not what I am conveying by any means. I am conveying God's intentions toward discernment found in the following scriptures:

- 1 John 4:1: "Dear friends, do not believe every spirit, but test the spirits to dee whether they are from God, because many false prophets have gone out into the world."
- 1 Thessalonians 5:21: "[B]ut test them all; hold on to what is good . . ."

- 1 Timothy 4:1: "The Spirit clearly says that in the later times some will abandon the faith and follow deceiving spirits and things taught by demons."
- Colossians 2:8: "See to it that no one takes you captive through hollow and deceptive philosophy, which depends on human tradition and the elemental forces of this world rather than on Christ."
- John 7:24: "Stop judging by mere appearances, but instead judge correctly."
- Matthew 24:24: "For false messiahs and false prophets will appear and perform great signs and wonders to deceive, if possible, even the elect."
- Psalm 119:125: "I am your servant, give me discernment that I may understand your statutes."
- Romans 12:2: "Do not conform to the pattern of this world, but be transformed by the renewing of your mind. Then you will be able to test and approve what God's will is— his good, pleasing and perfect will."

The aforementioned scriptures and several others throughout the Bible convey God's intent of discernment. It is a posture of revelation that comes through prayer, and it is designed to make us aware, equip us, and protect us. It is meant to keep us from becoming distracted and to allow us to guard against or watch for things that desire to derail us from destiny.

If you pay close attention, by discerning accurately, your success will reveal who's for you and who's against you. In his book *Leadershifts: Mastering Transitions in Leadership and Life,* Bishop Joseph W. Walker III writes,'

There are tons of folks in your life who embrace and affirm where you are now, because where you are now does not intimidate them or make a demand on them to change the dynamics of interaction with you. They are content where you are and where they are in the relationship. What you will discover is that once God shifts you into your "not yet," some will have difficulty adapting. (2014, 47)

Qualified in Prayer—A Systemic Covenant

The process of ascension and acceleration will require a change to your level of availability in some seasons. As God works to prepare you, there will be a need to become more available to God and less available to others. Those that truly love you, will understand when your degree of availability must shift. Those that use you, simply won't. God will often realign you to others that understand your pursuit of destiny. In those relationships, you will find less distraction and more development.

A good prayer to have is "Lord, help me to properly discern and evaluate my placement in relationships and in locations. Show me if I have internal hinderances and reveal to me external traps." The truth is the right people and places from several years ago may not be right for your now or your next. In Joseph's life, his immediate family caused friendly fire to occur. In Jesus's life, the concept of friendly fire came through those who served in ministry as teachers of the law/scriptures. He also encountered it through His disciple Judas.

Discernment postures your level of awareness. There is a threefold awareness you must possess to overcome friendly fire. The threefold awareness is rooted in the fact that God has qualified you. Understanding of your qualification is critical to your survival. This awareness is sealed in God's Sovereign systemic approach to how He qualifies. To obtain the victory during times of friendly fire, you must acknowledge the fact that *you belong to God, you are sent by God*, and *God equips you.*

Being qualified is systematic, or based in God's sovereign, intentional, covenant nature. When you are truly called by His

Name, the covenant will keep you from giving up on the journey to the top. Stay the course through prayer. Continue in intercession. Remain focused on the assignment He has called you to. When you belong to God, He cuts a covenant with you. When you are sent by God, He's right there in the midst of your situation. When God equips you, He sets provisions in place to sustain you.

Regardless of what comes against you, your qualification is sealed in Him! God has selected you to achieve prosperity and ordained your perseverance during times of intense attacks. In the midst of trials and opposition, you must remember whose you are. When you remember whose you are, the negative opinions of others cannot disqualify you from fulfilling your purpose. It doesn't matter who dislikes you. It becomes irrelevant who thinks you do not measure up, fit the criteria, or meet the requirements. The covenant you have with God has already qualified you!

The covenant you have with God is strong enough to keep you in the valley as well as on the mountain top. As I mentioned before, God has a vested interest in your success and ascension to the top! The blueprint is downloaded through prayer. Another revelation of Hebrews 5:14 is that God allows the testing during the valley experience to mature us as individuals:

> [S]olid food is for the mature, for those who have their powers of discernment trained by constant practice to distinguish good from evil." (ESV)

Ascend in Prayer—Capacity in the Valley

The reality of the valley is twofold: we are cultivated in the valley, and we gain a greater spiritual capacity in the valley. There are instances where God will allow a valley experience to expose those attempting to use you. The valley experience will sometimes be used by God to reveal individuals' true motive toward you. God will often use the valley to identify friend from foe. For this reason, wisdom says, "Do not invite people who could not support you or tolerate the calamity of your valley experience into a season of celebration."

Those who remain during difficult seasons are usually the ones that are found to be the most effective as it relates to being assets during seasons of ascension or elevation. They are an aid in retaining the right perspective during trying times and seasons of warfare. They are often the most valuable relationships as you pursue your purpose and define your destiny. They are the ones God uses to encourage you during the journey to the top. These are individuals with pure agendas toward you, and no unhealthy measures of envy exist in the relationship.

On your journey to the top, you will encounter friendly fire. Simply remember that God's plan for your life trumps any turmoil your enemies intend to create. Exercise reassurance in God and the ordained plan He has in place concerning you. As you do so, God's systemic intentionality will posture you in a place of victory despite friendly fire. This biblical truth was evident in both Joseph's and Jesus's life. Understand it still holds true today in your life as well. Refuse to become bitter, and allow the warfare of friendly fire to make you better. Discern and pray your way to the top in the midst of friendly fire!

~Warfare: Friend or Foe? End-of-Chapter Prayer~

Lord, I thank you for the ability to discern and overcome warfare. I pray for a supernatural release of divine strategy and spiritual insight during the seasons where I am engaged with friendly fire. I pray the angel of the Lord would be encamped around me and protect me according to Psalms 34:7. I decree the grace over my life to discern in accuracy. I declare eyes to see in the spirit in order to discern friend from foe. I thank You for hiding me in the secret place of the Most High and for causing me to abide under the shadow of the Almighty according to Psalms 91:1. I believe Your glory will be my defense according to Isaiah 4:5. I decree and declare that no evil will befall me, and no plague shall come near my dwelling according to Psalms 91:10. I thank you for deliverance from the hand of my enemies according to Psalms 59:1–2. Lord, I declare the grace is upon me to use the shield of faith to quench every fiery dart of the enemy according to Ephesians 6:16. I receive greater levels of awareness of who I am in You. I declare a receptive and strategic mind imparted and filled with Your wisdom, knowledge, and understanding according to Daniel 2:21. I am grateful for Your qualifying grace to live a planned life of purpose according to Jeremiah 29:11, and I receive Your promise of thoughts of peace and not of evil. In Jesus's Name, Amen.

Journal the Journey to the Top . . .

Chapter 8

THE APEX: YOUR MOUNT ARARAT

"Alleged 'impossibilities' are opportunities for our capacities to be stretched."

—Charles R. Swindoll

———————

AS YOU READ THIS CHAPTER, I NEED YOU TO KEEP a simple yet very powerful truth at the forefront of your mind. It's not about hoping your way into your apex, but rather it is the result of hard work and pressing past opposing forces. The

> No one stumbles upon greatness; it is planned, strategic, and a calculated result of hard work!

mistake many make is assuming hope is the essence of faith. They believe things will fall in their lap because they said so. Hope is a component of faith, not the essence of it.

James alluded to this spiritual concept in James 2:17 during his discourse on faith. The English Standard version of James 2:17 reads, "So also faith by itself, if it does not have works, is dead." The Message Bible gives a clear distinction between the language of faith and the corresponding action of faith. It reveals God-driven faith is not only in speech; rather, it requires a response or action. It reads, "Isn't it obvious that God-talk without God-acts is outrageous nonsense" (MSG).

God-driven faith, rooted in prayer, has a willingness, capacity, and ability to accomplish. Hebrews 11:6 informs us of the posture of faith that yields the ability to please God. It conveys this posture as one of action that leads to manifestation. The Bible says, "And without faith it is impossible to please him, for whoever would draw near to God must believe that he exists and that he rewards those who seek him." The ability to believe and seek allude to intentional acts. To "draw near to God . . . believing" is faith. Faith from the posture that He "exists" speaks of the ability to trust and expect what we are believing God for, He will accomplish. Expectancy must accompany faith in order to see results.

Manifestation is a result of the corresponding actions that occurred through faith. To seek is to go in search of in order to obtain. It speaks to a spirit of prayer and intentional intimacy with God. Faith that accomplishes or pleases God brings into existence an impactful reality. It's a posture where desire becomes real. In his book *The Secret Life of a #1 Salesman*, Solomon Hicks provides an evaluation of strategic planning and conveys the reality of intentional faith. He writes, "The willingness to do what it takes to get what you want is the only proof you have that your desire is real."

The Apex—An Elevated Perspective and Posture

At this point I feel it is important to clarify the significance of the chapter title. The apex is the place where you obtain the ability to look beyond self and your current situation. It is the place where your vantage point shifts due to elevation. At this point you are no longer feeling the weight of the valley. Instead, you feel the momentum of purpose and sense the ability to look beyond the burdens. Your mindset is not limited by impossibilities or distractions. This is the posture of truly embracing the affliction from the lens of purpose. This is why I had to open with God-driven faith. This is the place where our attention is toward the promise and we relinquish our will for His will.

The apex speaks of sustainability and the place of authority. God sustains us in adversity through His strength. The apex is a posture of heightened awareness. You are better because of all you've survived. It is a place where God's strength can be revealed through you and it occurs for His glory. The apex is a disposition of learning from affliction and maximizing the lesson. Bishop Neil C. Ellis addresses the blessing of embracing affliction in his book

Surviving the Crisis: "Adversity and affliction should be received as vehicles that compel us to look deeply into ourselves to see the new lessons we need to learn." (Ellis, 65)

The acceptance of adversity from the right perspective is the breeding ground for breakthrough in your prayer life. It opens you up in faith and expectancy for God to move on your situation. Praying in faith and expectancy is the catalyst to what I would like to call "your best is yet to come" season. The apex is the place of authority where I am fortified in faith that accomplishes.

In the apex, the shift from difficulty to destiny occurs because you have done the work to strengthen your desire and remain focused on God. The strengthening of your desire occurs and is birthed through prayer. Jesus said in Mark 11:24, "Therefore I say unto you, What things soever ye desire, when ye pray, believe that ye receive them, and ye shall have them" (KJV).

Perseverance and confidence are vital to achieving the level of greatness God has intended for you. The Amplified Bible's version of Mark 11:24 records, "For this reason I am telling you, whatever things you ask for in prayer [in accordance with God's will], believe [with confident trust] that you have received them, and they will be given to you."

The apex experience is about sustaining the momentum of perspective and perseverance. No matter how difficult or daunting the task, choose to persevere. The resilience you show in pursuing your destiny determines the magnitude of the impact you will make when it's achieved. The best is yet to come despite all the hindrances you may have faced. Do not limit your potential, and do not allow anyone else to do so either. No one should be allowed to admit you have potential and with the same mouth attempt to justify limiting your progress. Some people may never admit it or agree publicly with all that God has told you privately. It's okay. A private declaration from God always contains a promising destiny. Everything takes time.

The lesson we must learn about progress is that it comes with signs. Those signs must be viewed from God's perspective and not man's perception. Joseph's dreams were all signs of God's desire to progress him. Ironically, when Joseph shared his second dream with his father, who favored him over his brothers, the response received was from man's perception of Joseph's current situation. See Genesis 37:9–10.

There are several lessons to be learned from those particular verses. The main lesson in opposition as it relates to your potential and progress is God will provide indicators of progression. The lives of Jesus and Joseph reveal to us the favor of God does not necessarily require affirmation, instead His favor is revealed (or made known) through affirmation. Look for the signs through God's perspective and not man's perception. Your status as a dreamer will shift to visionary as you work the strategy to make your dream a reality.

The apex is a seat of focus and engaged potential. Potential is the qualifier for progress, the reason being God does not and cannot misplace potential. He is intentional behind all He does. Every talent and every gift God placed in you was released with purpose and intentionality.

Intentional in Prayer—Focused on Vision

Being designated by God to be successful, ascend, and live your purpose means you must be willing to be misunderstood. Some individuals you encounter on the journey to the top will be a great help to you. The rest will attempt to hinder, but you must remain purposeful and intentional about achieving your goal. Individuals become "okay" with you being successful when they can control the pace of your success. They become okay with the vision God has released to you only when they feel they can be credited with bringing the vision to life. It's vital to understand that a God-given vision is something you must own. Pastor Michael Slaughter wrote in his book *Momentum for Life,* "Visioning is a daily process of formulating and refining my own life calling." (2008, 88). Vision must be viewed as a promised destination that aligns with diligence and faith. You must become the greatest stakeholder in that vision. Pray it into fruition! Strategize a process to manifestation.

Dr. Cindy Trimm addresses our ability to maximize potential and manifest purpose in her book *Push.* She states, "You have not accomplished your goals, maximized your potential, written that book, started that business, or lost that weight only because you and you alone have decided not to." (2014, 95). To make progress in life, you need to surround yourself with those that challenge you without hindering you. Just as God was intentional about creating you for a purpose, you must also be intentional about obtaining the promise and living in purpose.

Resolving in your heart that God ultimately controls your success will cause you to thrive despite opposition. The role you play in your process of purpose is one of activity, not idleness. You must believe in yourself and the authentic abilities God placed inside of you. Several years ago, I was engaged in a discussion with one of my mentors. He told a simple yet powerful truth that shifted my view of success. He said, "Seek God for your niche. Don't be a generalist; be a specialist."

The moment you embrace the fact that God did not design and purpose you to stay in the shadows of others is the moment you will learn to stop apologizing for your growth. If you keep apologizing for the blessings and growth, then you'll remain bound to the opinions of others. This is a level of freedom and liberty that very few obtain. It begins with prayer and God revealing to you who you are in Him and Who He is in you! You will never truly enjoy life and any success you achieve until you allow yourself to be unapologetically blessed. Please know this is not a place of arrogance. It's an arrival to wholeness and satisfaction. The apex is a place of directed strength and no distractions.

Navigate in Prayer—A Covenant Mindset

The arrival into a place of elevation and expansion will happen for you! By faith, God will cause you to arrive to the place of promise no matter the test or trial you must encounter. I declare you will see the success God has in store for you! My earnest prayer for you is that you handle transitioning from your current situation into your God-ordained place of elevation in wisdom. Proper navigation is critical to obtaining and maintaining the place of promise. The perspective to grasp speaks toward realizing the opposition you've faced serves a purpose of impact toward elevation. Elevation and success come at a great price and can profit amazing results—if managed correctly. The area of caution when it comes to elevation and prosperity is once it is obtained, it is often misused or abused by some.

One of the saddest commentaries is for someone to work all their lives to achieve a status, level of recognition, or platform only to fall prey based on how they approach managing the decisions that come along with success. I don't believe anyone is above falling or failure, but I do believe God has equipped us to succeed without falling prey to any situation that will devour our achieved success. 1 Corinthians 10:13 states,

> No temptation has overtaken you except what is common to mankind. And God is faithful; he will not let you be tempted beyond what you can bear. But when you are tempted, he will also provide a way out so that you can endure it. (NIV)

I believe the equipping and the ability to choose "the way of escape" takes place in the posture of fervent prayer.

The posture of prayer is the posture of wisdom and insight. James addresses this in James 1:5. The scripture declares, "If any of you lacks wisdom, let him ask God, who gives generously to all without reproach, and it will be given him" (ESV). It's up to us to pray to God for direction and wisdom because it is possible to be in the right place but found making the wrong decisions. In most instances, frustration and the potential to fall is fostered in poor decisions.

Poor decisions primarily stem from emotionalism. This is simply a point of caution because when you surround yourself with people that are always in their feelings, you'll find yourself making decisions based on emotionalism in order to appease them. Being emotional is not necessarily a bad thing. It primarily becomes detrimental if we allow our emotions to consume our ability to accurately reason, discern (judge accurately), and pray.

Most pilots would agree the approach is vital to landing safely. Achieving prosperity in the midst of opposition is about approaching life with wisdom. The approach determines how you will land, and wisdom determines where and in what condition. To ensure you do not fall victim to any distractions that arise, you must choose to remain connected to God and consistent in prayer. This is a covenant mindset and a decision of discipline. It is rooted in intentionality of focus.

Wisdom in Prayer—Thrive without Distractions

A huge part of being successful and defining success for your life involves remaining focused, regardless of whether everything in your surroundings beckons you toward distractions. When elevation has found you, the strength of your focus is measured in two ways. First, how well do you handle distractions? Secondly, how well do you follow God's lead? To properly engage both areas and thrive in the apex, you must pray for His wisdom to be your portion.

The Bible conveys to us the worth of wisdom in Proverbs 8:11. The scripture says, "For wisdom is far more valuable than rubies.

Nothing you desire can compare with it" (NLT). It suggests the foundation of success or wealth—and retaining it—is wisdom. The wisdom of God will unction you to go where you are wanted and follow God to the place where you are needed. This is the disposition of greater influence and impact.

The wisdom of God will allow you to submit to God's leading and identify distracting situations you need to flee. This is evident in the life of Jesus and the life of Joseph. The ability to remain focused on the assignment is one of the primary keys to seize success. Joseph remained focused during his encounter with Potiphar's wife (Genesis 39:7–12), which afforded him the grace to flee. Jesus's ability to remain focused is made relevant in His discourse with Peter (Matthew 16:21–23; Mark 8:31–33) and more so in the Garden of Gethsemane.

The lives of Joseph and Jesus communicate the journey to the top requires a willingness to focus and walk in wisdom. It reveals you must be willing to reverence the assignment God has for you more than you value the opinions or acceptance of people. This is critical to thriving at the apex. To effectively navigate elevation, we cannot thirst after acceptance and be found willing to entertain and tolerate distractions. Although fellowship and forming a connection with others is a basic tenant of the Christian faith, on the journey to the top, you must remain balanced in your relational stance.

The reality is you cannot afford to embrace the concept of watering down who you are and who God intended you to be for the sake of acceptance. This is an important concept to recognize because it affords you the strength to shift when God leads you. Distractions and an inability to follow God's lead can leave you open to manipulation and undisclosed ill intentions. Embracing distractions can prove detrimental during your apex. Distractions and an inability to follow God's lead can limit your full potential and slowly suffocate potential during the journey to purpose.

When elevation has found you, living up to your full potential will reveal God's power to those you encounter. Cultivate the power in prayer. The place you currently reside in influence is not the final destination or intention of God concerning you. As alluded to throughout this book, God prospers us for an external purpose. The apex is the place of influence that impacts the external. The resolve to undertake is one that declares the benefits of elevation are designed to surpass your immediate circle and family. The apex is a place of kingdom influence and impact. Prayer must remain a constant to move in kingdom influence. The position of purpose is bigger than selfish gain.

Joseph makes this known in Genesis 50:20 when he says, "He brought me to this position so I could save the lives of many people." The impact of Jesus's obedience to God led to salvation. Romans 5:10 says, "For if while we were enemies we were reconciled to God by the death of his Son, much more, now that we are reconciled, shall we be saved by his life" (ESV). The process of elevation is not about self-glorification; it's about God's plan and purpose to impact the world through a willing vessel that operates life in God's wisdom.

Choices have guided your life, and that will not change once you obtain elevation. The impact of your decisions will carry greater impact and levels of influence. Being successful forces you to make choices at the next level. Success will demand you recover quickly, through repentance, from bad decisions. When elevation has found you, a mindset of grace must overtake you— the grace to recover from bad decisions and the grace to make wiser decisions come through prayer. This grace breeds the opportunity to relinquish guilt or condemnation.

Positioned in Prayer—The Press to Influence

When engaging growing pains, never make the mistake of classifying your pain as punishment. Pain is designed to bring forth your purpose. It is a powerful tool used to develop the passion toward the life God has predestined you to have. There is no failure when God is at the forefront. You may encounter opposition, but there is no failure! There's always something to learn, so resolve to grow through the opposition.

The pain in Jacob's hip during his wrestling match with an angel caused him to receive from the Lord. Paul's thorn in his side was intended to posture him in humility as God used him in extraordinary ways. Joseph's pain positioned him in status and favor that impacted his family for God's glory. Jesus's pain brought salvation, redemption, and power to believers. It qualified Him to be seated at the right hand of the Father (Luke 22:69) in a position of ultimate authority.

When pressing toward the mark in the midst of opposition, fatigue can set in. If it does, then it has the potential to stifle your progression by leading you to a false sense of contentment. The question the enemy may speak sounds similar to "why pursue the top if you are content?" I understand the Apostle Paul wrote about the need for contentment in the life of a believer (Philippians 4:11). The word *content* in verse 11 is *autarkes* in its original language, which means sufficient for one's self or to be independent of external circumstances. It speaks of joy in a current state, which does not equate to stagnation. This is important to understand because it informs us the contentment Paul referred to speaks toward personal internal satisfaction. The press and pursuit of the top is ordained for external change surpassing any one individual.

In other words, the God-reason and revelation behind pursuing the top is to position you in a place of influence and impact—similar to Joseph and Jesus. The journey to the top is about influencing lives. It positions us to become effective agents of change and ambassadors of God's agenda in the earth. For this reason, you must keep pressing to get to the top. Simply put, the assignment in you is greater than just you. The journey to the top is about the lives you will impact upon arrival. It is about His kingdom being revealed. Therefore, I beseech (beg) you: keep pressing!

A reality found within pressing toward the mark is it generates some measure of pain, but remember that the purpose behind the pain is closely connected to the promise. Those that do not understand your purpose and your promise usually have no idea of your pain or your pressing. Although you may feel like giving up, hang in there! God gives us strength to maintain during our weakest moments. The aforementioned is exactly why the Apostle Paul stated we ought to take pleasure in the weaknesses, hardships, and persecutions that we suffer for Christ—because when we are weak, then we become strong (2 Corinthians 12:10 NLT).

The pain you encounter en route to the promise is simply a gauge to determine the capacity of your promise. You must understand some will never really accept your rise to the top because of their current capacity and perception of who you are. But the more you endure, the more you can expect God to broaden your capacity to obtain the promise. In other words, the promise will prove to be worth all the pain you will experience or have experienced. Success, no matter how you define it for your life, breeds opposition.

When God ordains acceleration and growth concerning your life, expect opposition to increase. The good news is although opposition increases, you can expect God to increase the grace upon you to survive the attacks. He increases the grace in order for you to accomplish His ordained will for your life. When it's all said and done, the elevation and success that occurs will reveal God's glory in your life—similar to how your perseverance during opposition revealed God's grace and strength.

Contrary to popular belief, God does not invest into someone or something without expecting to receive a return on His investment. Therefore, because He has invested in you, you can expect things to take place in your life that will bring Him glory. The investment is meant to impact not only those closest to you but also those assigned to cross your path.

Destiny in Prayer—Commit to Stewardship of the Dream

Do not minimize your potential; it is the very thing that drives your possibilities. At times, as you press towards the mark, others will view your level of focus as arrogance. Joseph was able to see his dreams into reality because he did not sell himself short although he was the youngest child. He did not subscribe to the evident issues of the family structure that were present. He embraced the potential that his dreams revealed and held on to it. He held on to his potential when his parents would not receive God's plan for his life. He held on to his potential when his brothers plotted to kill him and sell him into slavery.

Joseph held on to his potential in prison as he pleaded his case because of accusations from Potiphar's wife. He pressed toward the mark by remaining committed to the potential revealed in his dreams. Retaining the potential can launch you into a place of possibilities. Remain committed as you press toward the mark. Your level of commitment will determine the level of your capacity and determine your corresponding action(s).

Jesus told a parable on stewardship that validates the importance of staying committed. Matthew 25:22–23 says,

> He also who had received two talents came and said, "Lord, you delivered to me two talents; look, I have gained two more talents besides them." His lord said to him, "Well done, good and faithful servant; you have been faithful over a few things, I will make you ruler over many things . . ." (NKJV)

Pressing toward your destiny requires stewardship. The essence of stewardship is embedded in faithfulness—not faithfulness to a platform or a position, but to God's agenda. Giving someone a platform will not retain his or her faithfulness. Faithfulness is an internal attribute of the heart God births in those He desires to empower to make an impact. An unfaithful heart is a destiny blocker.

For a believer, there cannot be a God-ordained impact in ministry or in life without a heart of faithfulness toward God's agenda. One of the keys to success, both spiritual and natural, is to obey what's on the heart of God and not the mind of man—this includes your mind as well. This is why the Bible urges us to trust in the Lord with all our heart and lean not (or do not depend on) our own understanding (Proverbs 3:5).

As you press toward making an impact, you must remember there is a reason behind the press. The reason for the press is attributed to the fact that your journey to the top will contain obstacles. Obstacles can cause fatigue. If you maintain the right perspective, then obstacles can provide momentum. The road to success, while managing trials and tribulations, is simply a matter of perspective.

Succeed in Prayer—Resilience: A Catalyst into Promise

Every difficulty you encounter is an opportunity to be successful and not to suffer. Your perception and perspective must remain resilient. God will cultivate your resilience through prayer and intercession. It's possible to be in the right place and receive the right opportunity. It's also possible to be in the wrong place and receive what seems to be the right opportunity.

Internationally renowned author and speaker in the fields of self-development and spiritual growth Dr. Wayne W. Dyer spoke toward the power of growing through life situations. He notes,

With everything that has happened to you, you can either feel sorry for yourself, or treat what has happened as a gift. Everything is either an opportunity to grow, or an obstacle to keep you from growing. You get to choose.

I often say that obstacles are catalysts to the anointing of God. Attempting to avoid an obstacle corresponds to a failure to embrace being anointed past your current state. This notion is alluded to during Jesus's prayer in the Garden of Gethsemane, when He prayed, *"[N]evertheless, Your will be done."* He realized forfeiting the cross would equate to forfeiting the crown and His position at the right hand of the Father as the Savior of mankind.

There are instances when God will direct your steps toward Pharaoh in order to elevate you. This proves true in the life of Joseph. An enlightened understanding of "Pharaoh" simply reveals the title represents an influential world leader. On the journey to the top, do not limit God's intent to elevate you. He is God enough to assign a "Pharaoh" to favor you.

Too often we associate Pharaoh with bondage, which was true in the Israelite's situation, but in Joseph's situation, Pharaoh was an instrument of elevation and favor. The term *pharaoh* is simply the title of an ancient Egyptian king. Scripture informs us in Proverbs 21:1, "[T]he king's heart is in the hand of the Lord, Like the rivers of water; he turns it wherever He wishes" (NKJV).

An expanded spiritual perspective exhibits God's power. God is omnipotent enough to use Pharaoh to bless you and bring you to a place of tremendous influence. Be careful of the cliché that solely associates Pharaoh with bondage. The reality is clichés make people excited, but they can be damaging to the God-encounter if not delivered via wisdom. Pressing toward the mark requires your ability to ignore the cliché and embrace wisdom. Joseph would have completely missed the plan of God for his life and family if he did not serve during Pharaoh's reign. The Bible says, "The

LORD was with Joseph, so he succeeded in everything he did as he served in the home of his Egyptian master" (Genesis 39:2, NLT).

Joseph's life and the life of Jesus tells us the favor of God will cause people to seek you out. The wise men and the multitude sought after Jesus, just as Pharaoh sought for Joseph. It's important to comprehend a title/position reveals that you have found favor with man. Possessing the anointing (or authority of God) worthy of your title/position reveals you have found favor with God. It's the anointing that breeds effectiveness in the position, not the title.

Favored in Prayer—Overcome, Conquer, and Impact

When God is forming you for the place of promise, no one needs to know your name but Him. He is the One providing divine favor and simultaneously orchestrating divine opportunities. People create opportunities for those they want; God creates opportunities for those the world needs. Pursue God opportunities. He is invested in your ability to impact lives.

The Lord may use others to release opportunities to you, but you must not view the individuals being used as the Source of the opportunities. Ultimately God is the Source. Outside of Him idolatry awaits. Where idolatry is present, pride is close by, and with pride comes the fall (Proverbs 16:18). That's how several may achieve the position, as it relates to reaching the top, but they often fail to fulfill their purpose with integrity. Compromising your integrity doesn't work. It dilutes the oil on your life and minimizes potency. Lacking integrity contaminates purpose.

God's process of integrity says do not gain a platform at the cost of purity because the process to prosperity (or elevation) requires clean hands and a pure heart (see Psalm 24:3–6). God gives us free will and yet requires our obedience. Therefore, we must be balanced and aware that obedience is faith driven and free will is pride driven.

Pressing toward the mark while navigating acceleration requires we remain committed to what God has called us to do. Our commitment is fortified through consistent prayer. The tenacity to press toward the mark is the mindset of an overcomer. Jesus addresses the anointing we possess through Him to overcome as we navigate trials and sorrows in John 16:33. The scripture says, "I have told you all this so that you may have peace in me. Here on earth you will have many trials and sorrows. But take heart, because I have overcome the world" (NLT).

This is a clarion call to remain encouraged regardless of life's difficulties. It's a charge to stay in a posture of covenant victory. Being called by God to salvation or to any position of betterment does not exempt us from trials. It does ultimately grant us the victory! We must resolve to press in our faith to conquer just as Jesus overcame the cross and the grave and Joseph overcame the pit and the prison. The conqueror is anointed to achieve in faith. Favor and faith are currencies of the kingdom. Destiny and greater grace are your portion. The anointing to overcome is maximized in a resolve to keep advancing. It is your time to arise and work toward what God has assigned you. Pray and continue to progress with momentum. Achieved possibilities await despite opposition! See you at the top!

~The Apex: Your Mount Ararat End-of-Chapter Prayer~

Lord, I thank You that my labor is not in vain according to 1 Corinthians 15:58. I give Your Name the glory, and I receive the confidence that He who began a good work in me will perfect it and see it into fruition according to Philippians 1:6. I decree that eyes have not seen, nor have ears heard, nor has it entered into the heart of men, all You have in store for me according to 1 Corinthians 2:9. I trust You to lead me and guide me into greatness and strategically position me in a place of influence and favor. I decree You have established my steps according to Proverbs 16:9 and Psalm 37:23. I declare my affections are set on things above and not on the opposition I encounter. I release the grace to decree a thing and it be established unto me. I thank You for the anointing to speak in faith and not doubt according to Mark 11:23. I thank You for an attentive ear, and I silence any voice that desires to speak louder than Yours. I thank You for an obedient spirit to act upon Your Word. I thank You for the anointing to sustain the Mount Ararat greater experience. I declare all that you have allowed me to achieve will not cause me to lose sight of You as Lord. I will not embrace everything the world offers and will not fall to the lust of the eyes, lust of the flesh, or the pride of life according to 1 John 2:16. I decree and declare Isaiah 41:10 is my portion. I will not fear for You are with me; I will not be dismayed for You are my God. I trust You to strengthen me and help me. I declare You will uphold me in righteousness with Your right hand. In Jesus's Name, Amen.

Journal the Journey to the Top . . .

_____

_____

_____

_____

_____

_____

_____

_____

_____

_____

_____

_____

_____

_____

_____

_____

_____

_____

CONQUERING OPPOSITION: NAVIGATING ACCELERATION

The "Five D" Concept

THERE IS A CONCEPT I DESIRE TO SHARE WITH you regarding how to navigate acceleration during seasons of opposition. It may seem basic to some but will prove to be impactful to others. The truth is there are times we know what to do but need it repackaged in a "new paradigm" before we can find the strength to embrace it. The first step in the process is to *Define*. At this stage, the goal is to strive toward providing a personal basis or definition of success. It is not simply identifying your goals; it's about defining them. This is primarily a period of self-transparency and self-reflection. It is strictly the foundation. At this point, there must be an internalizing of what success is for you. Whatever the answer, be sure to own the definition of success revealed. The definition will evolve as you grow and as your life's situations change. The journey to the top will cause you to evolve in thought and in life.

The next step during the process is to *Determine*. In this phase, you create and evaluate the necessary routes to your definition of success. An honest look at past successes and past mistakes is vital to making the necessary adjustments. As time progresses, the determine stage will test your level of dedication. There are some routes that will not lead to favorable results. In this stage, you will need to remain open to letting some things and some people go. Be willing to learn from mistakes. You will need to pray for direction and instructions.

The third stage is *Dedicate.* The dedication stage requires resilience. No one rises above adversity to gain success without maintaining a strong level of dedication to making progress toward his or her goal(s). Candid questions must be asked. For example, what level of sacrifice is required? Do I realistically see myself willing to invest time, money, sleep, and so on, and to what extent? Some of these questions can be asked at the onset (define stage) of your journey to the top, but they are more impactful during the dedicate stage because the answer to those questions in the define stage gives you a roadmap to where you want to go. During the dedicate stage, those same answers act to keep you working toward your desired end state. Remaining in a place of reinforced dedication is vital because it moves you into the next stage, *Diligence.* Reinforcement will only occur as you strive to remain persistent in prayer and intentional in efforts of execution.

The diligence stage is where the work of success takes place. It challenges us physically, spiritually, mentally, emotionally, and even socially. It brings us to a place of awakening as it relates to the "true level" of work required to obtain success. Some of this work will also be necessary in maintaining the elevation. The true level of work reveals those things we did not account for initially. This stage speaks loudly toward the possibility of physical fatigue, emotional stress, spiritual testing of your faith, mental weariness, and the social burdens of working toward success.

The diligence stage will be the most trying overall. It is the catalyst to launching you into manifestation and completion. The more effort you place on being diligent, the more likely you are to achieve sustainability. The fifth "D" is arguably the most vital because it is the stage that sustains and breeds momentum during each stage. It is not the last stage as it relates to importance or precedence. The *Devotion* stage is critical. It is the process of utilizing your placement in God to gain strength. This stage speaks toward meditating on God's Word and engaging God through prayer and intercession. The uniqueness of this stage is found in its subtle inclusion throughout the define, determine, dedicate, and diligence stages. Consistency through the act of devotion is a means of empowerment. It aids you in effectively navigating opposition on your rise to the top! God has called you to greater works (John 14:12). By drawing closer to God through prayer, you shall achieve them! No one can break what God has chosen to bless, and no one can hinder who God desires to help. Define goal(s), determine the necessary routes to achievement, remain dedicated to the process despite opposition, embrace diligence as a mindset, and be intentional about your devotion! See you at the top!

FROM THE BOTTOM TO THE TOP CATALYST TO CONQUERING:

Catalyst #1 ~ *You are called to accomplish and prosper!*

Catalyst #2 ~ *Guard your faith and your focus. Persevere!*

Catalyst #3 ~ *Establish a means of self-evaluation measured by God's Word!*

Catalyst #4 ~ *The path created for you is unique. Trust the promise God made you; trust His leading!*

Catalyst #5 ~ *Viewing the trial(s) from the lens of purpose will yield positive results!*

Catalyst #6 ~ *Forgiveness is the essence of a pure heart. Forgive your way out of hurt!*

Catalyst #7 ~ *Discernment is key to distinguishing friend from foe—internally and externally!*

Catalyst #8 ~ *No one stumbles upon greatness; it is planned, strategic, and a calculated result of hard work!*

Bibliography

Cottrell, D. (2006). *Monday Morning Mentoring: Ten Lessons to Guide You Up the Ladder.* New York: HarperCollins Publishers.

Ellis, N. C. (2004). *Surviving the Crisis.* Denver: Legacy Publishers International.

Hodges, K. B. (2003). *The Servant Leader: Transforming Your Heart, Head, Hands, & Habits.* Nashville: J. Countryman.

Jones, S. H. (2012). *The Secret Life of a #1 Salesman.* Acworth, GA: Hicks Global Enterprises.

Maxwell, J. C. (2017). *No Limits: Blow the Cap Off Your Capacity.* New York: Hachette Book Group, Inc.

McClendon, C. E. (2003). *Beyond Personal Power: Experiencing the "God-Kind of Faith."* Denver: Legacy Publishers International.

Morrison, M. A. (2008). *Compass: The Roadmap to Success for Ministerial Leaders.* North Brunswick, NJ: Marcia A. Morrison.

Morton, P. S. (2012). *Changing Forward: Experiencing God's Unlimited Power.* Nashville: Abingdon Press.

Murphy, W. H. Jr. (2019). *The Law of Prayer and Intercession.* Detroit: William H. Murphy, Jr.

Slaughter, M. (2008). *Momentum for Life: Biblical Principles for Sustaining Physical Health, Personal Integrity, and Strategic Focus.* Nashville: Abingdon Press.

Trimm, C. (2014). *PUSH: Persevere Until Something Happens through Prayer.* Shippensburg, PA: Destiny Image Publishers, Inc.

Walker, J. W. (2014). *Leadershifts: Mastering Transitions in Leadership & Life.* Nashville: Abingdon Press.

Walker, J. W. (2015). *Reset Your Life: Make a New Start.* Nashville: Thomas Nelson.

CONTACT US

FOR MINISTRY ENGAGEMENTS, TO BE ADDED TO our mailing list, or to enroll in the Ascension School of Prayer, Intercession, and Warfare online training, please contact us online at www.jerryaddyministries.org.

The Ascension School of Prayer, Intercession, and Warfare curriculum is designed to aid in the development and advancement of intercessors at all levels. It is structured to evolve within a Level I, Level II, and Level III track system.

The curriculum strategically builds upon itself with scriptural revelation and principles. It is designed to cultivate maturity and depth of revelation within those called to intercession or desiring a stronger prayer life. The curriculum examines key principles of effective intercession and provides insight to various aspects of an intercessor's, or person of prayer's, assignment within ministry and the kingdom.

Level I Courses

- Session 1—Clean Hands and a Pure Heart; *Part I: The Power of Repentance*
- Session 2—What is Prayer?
- Session 3—Understanding the Difference Between Prayer & Intercession
- Session 4—The Role of an Intercessor: Bridge the Gap
- Session 5—Being Led by the Holy Spirit

- Session 6—The Importance of Intimacy with God (Faith Focused)

Level II Courses

- Session 1—Flow in a Corporate Prayer Environment: *Discerning the Atmosphere*
- Session 2—Effective Positioning
- Session 3—Praying in Authority
- Session 4—Clean Hands and a Pure Heart; *Part II: Requirements to Ascend*

Level III Courses

- Session 1—Spiritual Discernment: *Accurate Movement and Momentum in the Unseen*
- Session 2—The Adversary and the Anointing
- Session 3—Engaging the Enemy Through Divine Strategy
- Session 4—The Breaker Anointing During Warfare Intercession

www.ingramcontent.com/pod-product-compliance
Lightning Source LLC
Chambersburg PA
CBHW051840090426
42736CB00011B/1901